Marshal Royal: Jazz Survivor

Also edited by Claire P. Gordon
Boy Meets Horn by Rex Stewart

BAYOU *jazz* LIVES

MARSHAL ROYAL

JAZZ
SURVIVOR

MARSHAL ROYAL

With
CLAIRE P. GORDON

CONTINUUM

NEW YORK ▪ LONDON

2001

The Continuum International Publishing Group
370 Lexington Avenue, New York, NY 10017

The Continuum International Publishing Group
The Tower Building, 11 York Road, London SE1 7NX

First published in Great Britain in 1996 by Cassell
by arrangement with Bayou Press Ltd

Printed in the United States of America

Library of Congress Cataloging-in-Publication Data

Royal, Marshal , 1912-
  Marshal Royal, jazz survivor / by Marshal Royal with Claire P. Gordon ; recording
chronology by Howard Rye.
     p. cm. -- (Bayou jazz lives)
  Includes discography (p.) and index.
  ISBN 0-8264-5804-1
  1. Royal, Marshall, 1912- 2. Jazz musicians--United States--Biography. I. Gordon,
Claire. II. Title. III. Series.

ML419.R68 A3 2001
788.7'165'092--dc21
[B]
                                                              2001047039

Contents

Editor's Note

Let me start by explaining how it happened that Marshal Royal and I collaborated on this book. We were both raised in Los Angeles from early childhood and while I don't recall ever having a conversation with him or Ernie "way back when", nevertheless we saw each other frequently in jazz venues around the city and we had a nodding acquaintanceship. Following the posthumous publication of Rex Stewart's autobiography which I edited, I wanted to help write an autobiography of another jazz great. I looked around for a local musician to work with and particularly thought of Marshal Royal. He was a world-class musician and it seemed to me that his reminiscences would include valuable data for future researchers about unknown and forgotten Los Angeles musicians.

It may surprise many people that early this century, before recordings or radio were available to spread musical concepts and ideas across the country, jazz was heard in Los Angeles. First-rate critics such as Leonard Feather have tried to dispel the myth that New Orleans was the sole birthplace of jazz. Marshal Royal's life is an example of a musician whose influences were neither New Orleans, Washington D.C., Philadelphia, Chicago nor New York. He was truly a product of the California jazz scene, having lived in Los Angeles from the time he was five years old. His story clarifies that jazz flourished in Los Angeles simultaneously with New Orleans.

My friend Sava Nepus, who knew Marshal better than I did, spoke to him on my behalf. Most likely he embellished my experience and abilities but Marshal was not persuaded immediately that he wanted me to do his book. At first he said that a few fellows had already approached him and anyway, since he wasn't too busy, he might just write it himself. His reluctance overcome, we began our sessions. Yet from time to time after we began he'd say, "I could do this myself, you know. It's no big deal. All I'd have to do is talk into a tape recorder and I'd have a book." This was not immodest. The fact is that Marshal was a very intelligent, articulate man and no doubt he could have written the book. But as I brought over pages of typed material, I think he came to realize how much work it would be.

As we taped, at times he would suggest that a particular recollection should not be included for one reason or another. In my opinion he'd now agree that those reasons are no longer valid so I will disclose a few of these opinions and recollections. They help tell his story.

Marshal's mother apparently had very light skin and the sort of fine features that allowed her to "pass" as white. He didn't wish this to be included because he thought people would construe this as bragging. He recalled that when he was a child, the department stores in downtown Los Angeles did not cater to an African American clientele. But Marshal's mother took him with her to a pricey, downtown store where she bought the family better quality clothing than was available in the local mama-papa shops. He especially remembered a beautiful Buster Brown suit, considered high style for a little boy at that time. From the many occasions that Marshal described uniforms and his clothing, I had the impression that he was concerned with his appearance, always wanting to present himself in an optimum way. I personally never saw him unshaven or unkempt.

He was named for his father and said he imagined that they were the only people in the world who spelled Marshal with only one "L". He had enormous respect and admiration for both his parents but particularly for his dad. Marshal Sr. was an officer in Los Angeles' black musicians' union (767) and was a fine musician who played and taught several instruments. Young Marshal emulated his dad by being a perfectionist about his playing and by unquestioningly accepting responsibility. As he entered his teens and began to earn money, he turned over most of it to help pay household expenses. Later, after his father had a stroke, unhesitatingly he took on the entire burden of supporting his family. He guarded and guided the career of his younger brother, Ernie. When it came to the welfare of his family, Marhal never uttered a word that made me think he resented shouldering these responsibilities.

It was not until he was in his thirties, when his mother,

sister and brother were all self-sufficient, that he felt able to marry. Without doubt this was a very happy marriage. Once when I was at the family home, his wife Evelyn recalled the first time she saw him. This would have been in the mid-1930's when Marshal made his first trip to Seattle with the Les Hite band. Evelyn took me aside and whispered that she pointed him out to a girl friend and said, "I'm going to marry that man." And so she did, many years later.

When I say whispered, let me explain. Evelyn had an affliction, probably cancer, which had required removal of her vocal chords. I was never told any of the details. The surgery left her with an opening in her throat. By holding a small appliance to it, the sound was amplified so she was able to use her breath to talk, but unfortunately only in a monotone. Surely losing her voice was traumatic for both of them, but Marshal was mum about such personal things. I only recall that he praised Evelyn as a wonderful vocalist, mentioned that she was older than he, that she didn't like to cook and what a good wife she was. Evelyn was in her 80's when she died of lung cancer only two years before Marshal.

The long stretches on the road away from home did not undermine this happy marriage, but certainly temptations abounded. As Marshal said, "There were the girls. Every night there was a bunch of girls out in front of the band stand just sort of begging for a date. They'd smile and wiggle a little. We got the message all right. Over the years I must have had about 1,000 women, all kinds. Dark ones, white ones, short ones, tall ones and all colors and sizes in between." But then he admonished me that this was definitely not to be included because, he said, "it would hurt her." He was very protective of Evelyn, very anxious not to have anything printed in the book that she shouldn't know. He went on to talk a little bit about two special women he'd met during the years with Basie. They were both "beautiful, smart, sexy." He thought he might have been happy with either of them. "But," he added, "my marriage was more important to me."

After his wife died, we spoke of doing more taping and adding some of the spicy material about life on the road. However about this time we were informed that the book was soon to be published. Unfortunately this convinced us that it was too late for any further sessions so even though the publication date was subsequently postponed, this material was not included.

Although Marshal read all the pages of the manuscript and made corrections as we went along, neither of us picked up on the fact that Ernie's wife was Florian Douceau in one place and her last name was spelled Duseau in another. He was an excellent speller and it may be that he didn't recall which was correct. I regret that at this late date it is not possible to determine which is the correct spelling and my apologies to the family.

Another discrepancy is the story about watching the *Normandie* burn in the harbor during the recording of *Flying Home*. Steven Lasker, an outstanding jazz historian, recently checked the recording date against the *Normandie* burning and discovered they were not the same! This is not to say that Marshal and the band did not watch the occurrence; just that it must have been a different session.

It was not Marshal's way to brag but his many fine qualities emerge in the book. He was a loyal friend, a dependable musician, always ready to assume responsibility wherever and whenever he was needed. He also had a few not so admirable qualities. He was not forgiving of offenses and slights. While he esteemed and was fond of many of his fellow musicians, it was quite clear that there were others he didn't care for and whom he disparaged. Some of this material was left out at his request.

One of the friends who became unpopular with him was Lionel Hampton. Prior to the forming of the first Hampton band in 1940, Marshal and Lionel had been fellow musicians with Les Hite. Some years later when Lionel was forming his first band, he hired Marshal to play violin and saxophone, and Ernie on trumpet. Marshal was unhappy when he discovered that Lionel had no music arrangements and that some of the young untried musicians in the group didn't seem to know how to tune up properly. He was also exasperated with Lionel's lack of judgment but quickly did what he could to get the band ready for their bookings. He did this as a friend and also just be cause it needed to be done. Instead of being properly rewarded, he writes about the conversation he overheard that motivated his leaving. It appears that he and Lionel were never friends again.

An example of his antipathy that was left out of the book occurred in 1990. I brought over Hampton's newly printed autobiography for him to read, hoping some incidents might refresh his mind. He looked incredulous and said, "Lionel didn't write this. The man can't write at all. If you gave him the 'A' and the 'T', he couldn't even spell cat!"

Generally, though, Marshal had kind words to say about everyone. Throughout the book the language and the words are almost entirely his own. My editing was primarily in selecting the sequence of material, eliminating redundancies, and tying various segments together. After speaking his thoughts and memories into my tape recorder dozens of times in 1989 and 1990, it is sad that in May 1995 he died prior to the publication of this book; it meant a lot to him that his autobiography was to be published. Now even though he is not here to read the book and the beautiful voices of his alto saxophone and clarinet are stilled, fortunately we have his memories and his recordings to validate the life and talent of this first rate musician. Marshal, you will not be forgotten.

Claire P. Gordon
Los Altos, California
May 1996

1
The Family

I was destined to be a musician. All my childhood, I was surrounded by music. From the time I was six weeks old, they tell me that I slept behind my mother's piano on my father's overcoat. "The Three Royals" was the name of a trio my parents and uncle formed in Texas. They were on their way to California when I was born on December 5, 1912 in the little town of Sapulpa, Oklahoma, sixteen miles from Tulsa.

I was the eldest of three children, and named Marshal Junior, after my father Marshal Royal, Senior. We seem to be the only people named Marshal who spell it with only one "L". My sister, La Verne, was born when I was four. Ernie was the baby, eight and a half years younger than I, born on June 2, 1921. He was named after Dad's brother, our Uncle Ernest. My talented younger brother became a very famous trumpet player. To my sorrow, he died a couple of years ago. More about him later.

The family arrived in California when I was five years old and I've maintained a residence here ever since so I consider myself a Californian. I remember 1918 very well, the year the Armistice was signed, because that's the year I started kindergarten. In those days, the educational system in California was very good. You could learn what you wanted to learn, if you wanted to learn. There were no problems excepting sometimes walking to school we had to cross streets that were practically entirely in mud. Back then, right after World War I, Los Angeles was still a small town and it was a different world from the way the city is today. It was almost like living in a small town. We didn't ever lock our front door and neither did anyone else.

My mother started teaching me piano when I was very, very little, about three years old. Naturally my hands were too small to reach octaves and she tried to stretch them for me. In the course of these sessions, I discovered that I already knew how the notes would sound! This is what is known as perfect pitch but I don't believe anybody actually has perfect pitch. I'd rather call it

1

approximate pitch, but it happens that I come as close as possible to having that ability. Despite my mother's efforts, I didn't have a deep feeling for piano and I think that was because it was my mother's instrument. I concluded that it was what ladies played and too feminine for me. Besides, I always had such a deep admiration for my father that I wanted to play the instruments he played.

Dad was born in 1878. He was a big man, rather handsome, six foot two and weighed around 250 pounds. He was jovial, the type of fellow who was well-liked by everybody. When I was about six, my father started me out on the violin. After Dad taught me for a few years and I had learned all that he knew to teach me, he had me take lessons from a woman violinist. Her name was Sinclair Murdock and she was a graduate of the Paris Conservatory. She was an astute lady with a no-nonsense European approach. Until I got into high school, I took one or two lessons from her every week, each an hour long.

During those growing up years, it seemed like times were always tough and we knew about a depression long before the stock maket crashed in 1929. By the time I was twelve, I'd been playing violin for about seven years so I played pretty well. I wanted to earn a little money to help out at home but I could not work anywhere legitimately because I was a minor. However, there was one way. Most of the movie theatres had stage shows with professional talent and they also put on amateur contests. These were a big draw and it seems like every theater in Los Angeles had one, and each theatre had its own amateur night. I'd get the line-up on all the theaters in various areas of Los Angeles and know where the contest was being held on any given night.

Then I'd take my violin and, on Monday night for instance, I'd go out where they were having the contest. I'd walk there if it was close enough or else take the street car. Luckily, the streetcars ran until midnight or so and it was safe to be out at night alone. No one molested children in those days. When the contest started, I'd get up on stage with my violin and play some popular song that everybody liked. After everybody had performed, the MCs would put their hands over the head of the contestants and the audience's applause would determine who won. The winners got a prize, usually money. This would be about fifteen dollars for a first prize, ten dollars for a second and about five dollars for third. That was a lot of money in those days. Some breadwinners in families only made $18-20 a week.

On Tuesday, I'd go way over on the other side of town where they didn't know me. Then Wednesday night I'd enter the contest in still another theater and so on, right through the week. I'd actually almost be working regularly by going from theater to theater. After I had done this for several months, they got to knowing me in the different areas and started to bar me from participating because they claimed I was really a little pro, making a business of amateur contests. They'd say, 'He's too slick, the kid is a pro." This prevented me from making a living, because I usually won first prize and I was earning $75-$100 a week!

While I was in school, my mother made sure she went through all my report cards and my home work and so on. She always kept me in line and was on top of things including being involved with the Parents and Teachers Association. That's because schooling was very important in our family. Mother's family was involved with education. Her father built the first schools for blacks in Denison, Texas, where she was born (née Ernestine Walton). His wife, my grandmother, had studied to be a teacher at Wilberforce College. And my mother, too, had been a school teacher. During my childhood, she, my father and my uncle were all music teachers, giving lessons on several instruments.

We were a very close knit family. Uncle Ernest was the same as a father to us. There were only the two sons in the family and they were always very close. In effect, we three kids had two fathers, like one big family. We lived in a four bedroom house. And just behind our house there was another house where Uncle Ernest lived and had a studio for his music pupils.

My mother came from a big family and she was one of six children, with three brothers and two sisters. Her father, Willoughby Walton, besides being involved with education, bred race horses. He had a string of predominately grey horses and went to Hot Springs, Arkansas every year to sell the foals at auction.

In my eyesight, my mother, Ernestine, was a very beautiful lady and most people would agree. She was very light-skinned, small and slender when she was young and stood just over five foot two. But, after having three children, she became rather hefty. She was a sweet woman, very motherly, very caring for her children.

My parents were upright people, strict about my learning right from wrong. Like most black people, the family was religious but it was Uncle Ernest who was most serious about religion. He was very devout and took me along with him to Christian Science church every Sunday. When I was young, he enrolled me there and I attended services for several years. Gradually, he convinced my mother about Mary Baker Eddy's teachings. In the early 20s she switched religions. She and my sister attended Christian Science services and Mother even became a Christian Science practitioner. In later years, Uncle Ernie got connected with a religious group called Father Divine. He moved to New York and lived there in Father Divine's temple until he died. However, my dad did not change his childhood Protestant religion and remained a Methodist all his life.

June 27, 1927 is a date I'll never forget. It was the day of my graduation from junior high school. After getting my diploma, Uncle Ernest came up the line with a gift. He was a little over six feet tall, very thin, and he had had an accident as a young man which left him with his left leg stiff at the knee. He walked up to me stiff-legged and handed me a little box.

"What's this?" I asked him.

"This is your clarinet," he told me. "You're going to be a clarinet player, and I'm going to teach you. When you start high school in September, you're going to be the first clarinet player in the band."

I was dubious and responded, "Oh am I?"

And he answered with assurance, "Yes, you are!"

My father had taught his younger brother how to play instruments and now he took it on down the line and decided to teach me. That summer, every time I started to run out to the

YMCA or the playground, Uncle Ernest had his arm on my shoulder and said, "You are coming my way," and so I was in for two or three hours of clarinet practice every day at his place. The complete summer, all of July, August and the first part of September, there were lessons every day except Sunday when he took me to church.

Adjusting to the clarinet from the violin was not a big problem. By then, I was sufficiently accomplished on the violin that, while I was still in junior high school, I had been selected to play in the Junior Philharmonic Orchestra! Changing instruments was just a matter of me adjusting to the fundamentals of playing and fingering the clarinet and developing an embouchure. So I progressed on the clarinet in leaps and bounds and it took no time at all for me to be playing fairly well. Uncle Ernie was right! After that summer of daily lessons, I really could play the clarinet.

In 1928, some people with a new supermarket came to the high school and inquired in the music department if they could get some young fellows to play at the opening. At the time, I was the concert master playing violin at Jefferson High so I was the one who got the call.

"Could you get a group of fellows together?" they asked me. "We'll want you to play 3 hours or so and you'll be well paid for it."

At that time, supermarkets were an innovation and these openings were grand affairs with free samples, balloons, music and all that. This particular market was way out in a sparsely populated area called South Gate. They wanted a saxophone, violin, trombone, a bass or a piano, I can't remember exactly whether there were to be six or seven of us, but it was just to be a small orchestra. I answered "no problem" because I had already played professionally several times on the violin with my family's orchestra.

Usually, this "orchestra" was just the three of them; my mother, father and uncle. Each of them could double on many instruments. My dad played clarinet, alto saxophone, C-melody sax, banjo and guitar. Uncle Ernie was just as versatile, he played both the reeds and the trumpet . Mother played piano and they all

5

sang. From the time I was twelve years old, I occasionally worked with them as an addition to the orchestra.

Sometimes, I was taken along to the studio to work on a movie. Back in those days of silent pictures, the studios used music to inspire the feelings which the actors were supposed to portray. These were known as "atmosphere" musicians, playing mood music behind the scenes. This was all ad lib, no written music, just according to how we understood the mood and according to our repertoire. My dad did a lot of this kind of work and sometimes he took me along to play mood music on the violin, too, starting when I was about fourteen years old. This would just be a day or two, doing a few special scenes with the stars.

I recall an engagement when I was hired by Miss Alma Hightower. She was Alton Redd's aunt and also played drums. She taught children, had a kid band and was one of these people who knew how to round up jobs to play. This particular job was 50-60 miles out of Los Angeles in the Country club at Lake Narconian. She hired a driver to take us there in a car. I was only about fifteen years old at the time, the youngest musician there, as this particular engagement was for an all adult group. Our driver was a young red-haired fellow, a couple of years older than me. His name was Red Mack and this is when I first met him.

Red was still just learning to play trumpet at that time. Like a lot of young people learning an instrument, he always had his horn along with him. He was invited to sit in with the band that day and it was the first time he had played with any kind of orchestra. It seems to me that most young trumpet players of that time were trying to mimic Louis Armstrong. Red tried to sing and talk and play like Pops Armstrong. His voice even got hoarse from trying to imitate Louis. Over the years, he got to be known around town as a good trumpet player with his own style. Later on, about the mid 30s or so, I recall that he was hired by Will Osborne, who led a white orchestra, to do a tour out of Los Angeles. It was still pretty unusual for a white band to hire a black musician at that time.

Aside from these few jobs with small groups but mostly with my family, I had never been allowed to play with anyone else because I was a minor. Besides they didn't want me to become involved with anything that wasn't just right. There were things you could get involved with in those days, too.

I went home and told my father about the supermarket opening job and that they wanted a saxophone player. Dad, who had all the horns, took me in the back room and taught me to play the saxophone that afternoon, on an alto. He showed me how to play a chromatic scale, which encompassed all the notes from the bottom of the horn to the top of it. Then he showed me where the octave key was to play one octave higher. I practiced all that evening and again the next day after I came home from school. The following day was Saturday when the market was scheduled to open. At that time, the clarinet was still pretty new to me. I had only been playing it six months or so. About four months after I had started out on the clarinet, I switched over from violin and was able to play all of the popular tunes of the day on it. So, for that market opening, after that little bit of practice, I was able to play the saxophone with the group. As I recall, the side men were each paid five dollars and I got ten dollars, which was a top salary at that time. Right then, I started being a saxophone player. For me, clarinet was the transitional instrument from violin to the saxophone.

All the schools I attended, from grammar school on, were on the east side of Los Angeles. The years I went to Jefferson High, the area wasn't really a black community. Only about 20 % of the school enrolment was black, which we called "colored" at that time. The rest was a mixture of Jewish, Japanese, a few Russians and Latinos and some just regular Caucasians, too. There were no black teachers in the Los Angeles school system then. I enjoyed myself in high school because there wasn't a whole lot of different prejudices such as goes on now. The prejudice was there, but communications were a little bit different in that area.

Music was my first love, but sports were a close second. At Jefferson High, all the guys tried all athletics. Everybody played baseball and football. The only thing I didn't play much of was basketball because I was too short. I got tired of the big guys banging me on top of the head. All my life I've followed athletics

7

including doing a little amateur boxing. This my father immediately eliminated once he found about about it.

"You'll ruin your fingers," he warned. "You are nuts to try to hit somebody on their hard head when you are a violin player" and that was the end of that.

I still follow sports and, since I was very young, I have enjoyed going hunting and fishing. My mother's brother was an outdoor man all the way, an avid hunter and fisherman. His name was Dave Walton, but we called him "Unca Pat." At an earlier time, this uncle drove cattle at the end of the Chisholm trail, going from Texas all the way to Montana. He settled in Montana and raised his family there.

I first saw him when I was a little guy, about five years old when he came out to visit us. He gave me my first watch, an Ingersoll pocket watch, so I never forgot him. Later, when I was about fourteen, he and the family moved to the Los Angeles area. From then on, he would take me hunting and fishing whenever we had a chance. Unca Pat would rather hunt and fish than wake up in the morning! He was a good looking, brown-skinned man who worked as a postal employee and, although he didn't play any instruments, he taught me a lot and is responsible for my life-long interest in being an outdoor man.

All those years, my Dad worked in many ways with his music. He was an orchestra player at parties given by the very, very rich Angelenos and the Hollywood crowd. He was hired by important people like Marco Hellman of the Hellman National Bank (which merged with the Bank of Italy to become the Bank of America). We'd go up to Ventura County to the Conejo ranch, which was the biggest ranch in this area, and they would have big barbecues etc. At that time Dad would get paid fifty dollars a day for himself. He was able to pay his musicians twenty-five to twenty-seven dollars a day, which was a tremendous salary then. I remember the first time I worked on a big time job for my father's group, I got twenty-seven dollars and fifty cents, just like the other men. This was at a time when the average pay was about two dollars a day!

My dad stayed busy. There was his work in the silent films

as an atmosphere musician playing mood music and he was called regularly. Now and then he also did little parts with people like Mae Murray, both acting and playing. And on top of that, Dad also was a music teacher. Giving lessons on all the instruments he played was a major source of his income. He taught me to play banjo and a little bit of guitar, too, which gave me my chord knowledge. When I started high school in 1927, I began a music course in harmony. For the whole four years, I studied harmony and actually got into scoring and writing at that time.

Although my father was always working and making good money, we weren't poor, but we weren't rich, either. We didn't have five or ten thousand dollars in the bank and we didn't own our home. We lived in a nice, rented two story house with four bedrooms, as nice a house as there was in that area. My father spent all the money he made on his family. He wanted the best for us, so he'd go to the butcher store and cut his own meat. We always had steaks on our table. My dad was also a great cook. We children were well-dressed, always clean and decent. Mother dressed my little sister beautifully and bought me Buster Brown clothes. This was the name of a company known for making high class children's clothes. That's the way my parents tried to raise us children and that was the reason the family had come to California, he explained to me.

He wanted to come out west, he said, so we would have a better life than you could have in the south. He wanted to make sure that we children could get a decent education, which had been such a hard struggle for him. In order for my dad to learn to play instruments correctly, he had to take a job at Kit Key college for women in Texas, working as a cook and waiter. The school had a very fine music teacher who agreed to give him lessons at night after Dad had finished all of his daily duties. The teacher taught him harmony, arranging, how to read and write music, and to play clarinet as well as many other different instruments.

After he had learned as much as he could, Dad went back home to Sherman, Texas and taught most of his friends in the neighborhood. He was a very successful teacher and instructed enough local people to play that they could form an orchestra. My

9

father became famous in his home town for creating musicians. After he left there, and possibly even before, a street in Sherman was named after him called Music Street. Incidentally, Buddy Tate was born in this same town.

Dad managed to see quite a bit of the United States before he settled in Los Angeles. He worked on the Mississippi Riverboats, had a band in 1892 at the St.Louis World's Fair and happened to be in San Francisco in 1906 for the big earthquake. My father never forgot that he had to get his education the hard way, by working in a menial job. He used to tell me, "As long as you live, son, never go back down south!" I was a child who could understood what he meant. I never went down south until 1940 and my father was dead then. When I got there in the 40s, things were still pretty bad in Texas or any other part of the south and I found out exactly what he had been talking about.

My father worked hard and was ready to relax when he got home. He never used any kind of drugs but he did take an occasional drink of bourbon and water. I never saw him drunk and I don't believe he ever did get drunk. From the time I was a small boy, he would always give me a taste, too, whenever he was going to have a drink. He'd give me maybe a teaspoon full because he wanted to make sure that I knew what liquor was, that it wouldn't be a mystery to me so I would be able to take it as it came. It turned out that my dad taught me well and I've never been a drunk, either. I can drink anything if I start and if it's something I like. And if I don't like it, I don't touch it.

I admired everything my dad did. He was like the lord to me. As a father, he couldn't possibly have been any better, so naturally I grew up trying to emulate him. And my mother was a very loving person. When I hear about the tough childhood some people had, I realize how very, very fortunate I was.

Mother would have about died if she'd ever caught me taking any kind of drugs and that includes using plain old marijuana. In those days, marijuana grew out in the open every place in Los Angeles, in the alleys, out in the fields and all over. Little kids will pick a plant, anything that's green and start smoking it out behind the garage. Sometimes we were smoking marijuana and didn't even know anything about it! I tried it a couple of times when I was younger but I never liked it because I don't care for anything that slows me down. I'd tell my friends that I didn't smoke grass and they'd answer that the least I could do would be to light it up for them. So I'd light up and pretend like I was smoking it, too. But even pretending, I would start being affected and got the feeling that I was being slowed down. I didn't want that.

Actually, I avoid anything that changes me. I've never even taken a sleeping pill. I figure if I'm sleepy enough, I'll sleep. And I never took a wake up pill, either because I'm afraid that if I ever got to the place where I needed something to wake up, I'd start taking something else, too. My concern started when I was growing up. There were times when I was working at the movie studios that I saw some young people almost turn into vegetables from amphetimines. The pills were given to them legitimately, by registered doctors, so they could continue making their appearance on the stage and screen. I wouldn't mention a name under any circumstances but I saw it and it was pointed out to me. That was a good lesson for me; I've kept away from drugs.

It's worth mentioning that we had a few famous people who came out of Jefferson High school. Perhaps the most noted person would be Ralph Bunche, who grew up to be United Nations Secretary. He was one of the first important blacks in that area. We were all pretty poor, no one could afford university when Ralph Bunche graduated from Jefferson, but he was subsidized to some extent. Some black people in the area who had a few extra dollars in their pockets gave this man a chance to go to college even though things were tough. People in the black community were really the first ones to know about the depression. Four or five years before the crash in 1929, we already had money problems.

2
I Go To Work

I worked with my parents only up until 1929 or so when the big crash happened. Then, nobody had any money anymore so they allowed me to accept outside jobs. At that time, I was only sixteen.

Not counting my parents' group, the first big band that I played with was Leon Rene. His claim to fame is that he wrote the song, *When the Swallows Come Back to Capistrano.* Later, he devoted his time to publishing and making records. A few of my older school mates had grown up and were now young men, playing in this very good group.

Originally, Rene's group had two saxes and one trumpet but when I came in I was added as a third saxophone in that group. The other saxophone players with Leon Rene were Charles Jones and Marvin Johnson. In school, all three of us had played in the senior orchestra. Marvin was also an alto saxophone player, had a nice tone and was a good student of his instrument. He was a great admirer of Johnny Hodges and could copy many of Johnny's solos note for note. It was Marvin Johnson who recommended me to Leon Rene.

Years later I was able to return the favor. It was about 1940 when Count Basie came through Los Angeles and asked me to join his band but I couldn't make it. The way it was slips my mind. Either I had promised Lionel to go with him or maybe this happened when I was already with Hamp. Anyway, I suggested Marvin instead, Count Basie hired him as second alto and he went to New York with the band.

The other saxophone player I had also known since my early school days. When I was in second grade, Charles Jones was one of the older fellows that I admired because he played good baseball. He wasn't playing an instrument yet when we were in grammar school. Later on, we were both at McKinley Junior High School at Vernon and McKinley. Charlie was a very attractive fellow, well liked by everyone both for his appearance and his nice personality.

Some people thought we three saxophone players were brothers because we worked together so often and for many years. Marvin and I looked very much alike although he was a few years older than I. We were the same height and size and resembled each other even to having the same kind of little moustache.

Later on, Charlie married Grace Morgan whose family owned the biggest funeral parlor for blacks in Sacramento, California and he left music. He and Grace had a son, Charles, Jr. and a pair of twins. When Charles, Sr. passed a few years back of cancer, his widow inherited the business and is now the sole owner. She still makes sure everything is correct in the business, which has expanded enormously, and these days it is these sons who are running the funeral parlor.

After I had been with Leon Rene for a few months, I left to work in one of the highest paying jobs in town, playing for a bandleader named Atwell Rose, who was also a violinist. The way this happened was that one Sunday, Atwell invited me to go along with him to his violin lesson and to meet his teacher. Rose was taking lessons from a noted classical teacher named Zoellner, whose family had a string quartet.

After that day, Atwell Rose knew that besides violin, I could also play the saxophone. One way and another, I suppose the word had got around. This could have been the confusion of my having the same name as my father and our playing the same instruments. There was always a question of differentiating who was meant in a conversation. Was it Marshal Royal Sr. or Marshal Royal Jr.? I was never called "junior" and when I was only sixteen years old, I was considered one of the leading sax players in town. Even though I was under the legal age to work, Rose invited me to join his group. This job was at a 10¢ a dance place in downtown Los Angeles.

Atwell Rose was a little guy, about five feet five, a quiet, intelligent fellow who read a lot and was very studious. He continued to study the instrument diligently all of his life. He played violin in a glorious manner, and was probably the best violin player among the blacks in Los Angeles, the best we ever had. While he was never the hottest jazz player, when it came to playing legitimate violin, he was every bit the violinist that Eddie South was in the east.

The Atwell Rose job paid $50 a week, which was big money then. This made it possible for him to attract some exceptional musicians for his orchestra. There were four horns in the group. Our trumpet player was Harold Scott, we had Lawrence Brown on trombone, the tenor saxophone man was Carlton Wade and I was on alto.

Carlton was a fellow who had migrated from Arkansas or Texas with his mother. She was quite well-to-do and always saw that Carlton had the best of everything: the best clothing, best instrument and best automobile. He had sports cars at a time when it was unheard of for people to own a sports cars bought right out of the show room. I remember he picked me up and took me to work in his Moon, which was a car that they stopped making at the end of the 'twenties. His mother bought it for him with cash.

You'd think he'd be spoiled, but he was one of the nicest guys that anybody every met. He was almost continuously happy and smiling. I suppose it helped that he had absolutely nothing to worry about. Unfortunately, his health failed him and he died at an early age.

Previous to joining Atwell Rose, Carlton played with the Charlie Echols band. Charlie Echols was a trumpet player in town and quite an extraordinary person. He didn't really know that much about trumpet but he had an enormous range for playing high notes. Many times he would play a high note just because the high note was there, not necessarily because it should be included in the tune or the formation of the chord. But he was a showman. He always fronted the band and hired as many good musicians as he possibly could. Some of the men who were in his orchestra at one time or another were Don Byas, Jack McVea, Teddy Buckner, and whoever else was around that was a good musician.

Charlie Echols was a very handsome man but also a pretty rough character, very strong physically and an excellent street fighter. His band played mainly in the night clubs where they had shows. For a time, they were working at a club owned by Billy Papke, who was the middleweight champ of the world in the early 'twenties. Papke's club always featured black entertainment, a line of girls who sang and danced and an orchestra. Quite a lot of the clientele who frequented Papke's club were sailors and from time to time, some of them got boisterous, out of line, or said the wrong thing. When that happened, if you'd looked up to the band stand, you'd find out that Charlie Echols had disappeared. He'd be down in the middle of the dance floor proceeding to knock out cold whoever the boys were who had been obnoxious. He would take on one, two or three at a time. Charlie was a fast fighter. Nobody ever knew how long he could last, but he was one of the fastest you've ever seen.

Charlie Echols was unique in his style with the ladies. If he had one girl friend, he must have had a hundred. Somebody said that he was a great lover and the word sort of spread around town. I'm not exaggerating when I say that he had a least a hundred girl friends, and they were all good lookers. In those days we didn't have hotels or motels or places like that to take a lady, but when he finished his job at night, Charlie would have two, three, or four rooms reserved in the neighborhood. He'd go from one place to the other, two, three or four of them the same evening, each and every night, to visit his girl friends. This kept his reputation as a great lover going very strong. Sadly, while still in his prime he became ill and had to be hospitalized for good.

Alton Redd, Jack McVea, Paul Campbell and a few other fellows were working for Charlie Echols in Long Beach. Sometimes the fog got so thick in those days between Long Beach and Los Angeles that you could barely see the road. Visibility would be down to about ten feet. One of the things we used to laugh about was the time these fellows were driving home down Long Beach Boulevard in one of those terrible fogs when, all of a sudden, they could just barely make out a grey horse in the mist. They were already so close it was impossible to avoid hitting it. They demolished the car and killed the horse. That was a strange happening, to hit a grey horse in a fog!

In Atwell Rose's band, Alton Redd was the drummer and

Harold Brown, Lawrence's brother, was on piano. It was an excellent group. At the time, there were several dance halls and we were working at a dime-a-dance hall on Main Street between 2nd and 3rd. During school hours, I tried my hand at writing a few little arrangements for the band. Then, to get my homework done, I memorized the work book so I wouldn't have to look at the music while I played at night. That way, I could do my school assignments on the band stand. At the dance hall, the saxes would play one chorus then the brass had the next one. I sort of learned to speed read during the time the brass had their turn. I could finish half a book during the period of an evening. This was practically the only time I had, because on Sunday I worked at the theaters with live music on stage. It was rough but I managed to get through school with pretty good grades, anyway.

Once, though, I just couldn't find enough time. The assignment was to read a book and then write a report about it. In order to turn in a paper, I invented a book I had supposedly read. It was, as I recall, a Western story. I created the plot, a name for the author, and so on. When I turned in the book report, the teacher questioned me about it and I finally confessed that I had made the whole thing up. After that, she sent me down town to have an IQ test. They told me that I scored pretty high and I thought about going to college, which is what my mother wanted me to do. When I graduated from high school in 1930, I was only a half credit short for college. But in those days, it was very rough to work and also attend a university. Even though my mother always hoped I'd become a doctor or a lawyer, it was too great a burden to put on my family to afford for me to stop working. Actually during those Depression years, my salary was very much needed at home.

While I was in the last year of high school, Lawrence Brown and I made a change together. By then, I had known Lawrence for quite a while. I first heard him play when he was with Paul Howard's Quality Serenaders. The leader, Paul Howard, was one of the first in Los Angeles and he played tenor saxophone and clarinet. He was an excellent musician who had studied music in his home town of Steubenville, Ohio. His orchestra had the

16

distinction of having special arrangements written for them when this was exceptional. He hired the better type musicians in town, the excellent readers as well as men who could take off and do their own solos. All of this helped to validate the orchestra's name "Quality Serenaders".

When I was still a kid, the Quality Serenaders were playing at a night club called the Hummingbird in the black area, at 12th and Central. This was a small club which had no bar, as these were prohibition days. I had to sneak down there to hear them because there was a strictly enforced curfew in those days for young people in the Los Angeles area. But I took the chance and went anyway because they were just about the elite of black orchestras of that day.

My parents knew what I was going out for: to listen to music, which was a big part of my life. They had no objections and all they asked was that I let them have an idea of where I would be. Mom and Dad respected me as having enough sense to take care of myself. I knew I was safe walking on the streets at night. There was never a question of anything happening to me, because nobody bothered children in those days, and I wasn't going to bother anybody else. Besides, I knew somebody who lived on practically every street which I had to pass walking from 12th Street to 34th Street going down Central Avenue.

As far as the curfew was concerned, I just had to be careful to keep the law from picking me up. The fact was, I had been working as a minor ever since I was twelve years old, which was not in accord with the laws, either. So being too young and too small to go inside didn't stop me. I used to hang around at the side of the building and listen to them play.

I wasn't the only one sneaking out at night those days. In order to go to work, Lawrence actually had to leave his house without permission. His father was a minister and wouldn't allow his sons to be in a night club. And that was where both Lawrence and his brother worked!

The first time I ever worked with Lawrence was when I joined Atwell Rose and we were playing at a penny dance hall called Danceland. The job ended suddenly when the joint was closed after a riot. One night, the Filipino customers fought with knives and somebody stabbed the owner during the free-for-all. Now, we both went to work at a club called The Apex on Central Avenue for Curtis Mosby. Earlier, in 1926, the Lincoln Theater opened in Los Angeles at 23rd and Central. The leader of the pit band was Curtis Mosby, who put the band together and played the drums. He was a little bit on the hefty side and, although he knew very little about music, he was a very good man at forming bands and getting jobs. He had some excellent musicians in that pit band including Les Hite. But I didn't meet Les then, because in 1926 I was still a boy and I actually never met Les until I went to work for him later.

The Mosby band only stayed in the pit of the Lincoln Theater for about a year or two, because having a big band was quite an extravagance at that time. But Curtis Mosby was a tenacious man with a lot of push. He actually didn't have that much on the ball as a musician but had become a bandleader because he was a businessman who knew how to make something happen. A lot of times in doing so, he ran out of money and wasn't able to pay everyone. But he persisted and eventually turned out okay. In his later years, long after I had left his band and when everyone thought he was down, he married a woman who made a lot of money in cosmetology. She pulled him out of his doldrums during the war by she helping him to open a place on Central Avenue called The Last Word. It was across the street from the Club Alabam and quite successful.

Going back to when I played with him, Curtis Mosby was running the Apex Club and his band was called Mosby's Blue Blowers. He was fronting a 10 piece group, which was considered a pretty good size at that time. Lawrence and Sonny Craven were the trombones. One of the saxes was Johnny Mitchell, who actually made most of his money teaching saxophone, clarinet and violin. On top of that, on the side he had a plastering business, working with cement. Leo Davis, another saxophone, was one of the better players in the Los Angeles area. He was originally out of Arkansas. The first time I saw him was when he was working with Mosby in the pit orchestra of the Lincoln

Theater as the lead sax, and also playing clarinet. He was a very capable musician, had a good tone, played solos, and knew how to play his horn correctly. I came in to replace Willie Griffin, who had taken sick. Johnny Mitchell, Leo Davis and I, on alto, were the three saxophones and all three of us doubled violin.

James Porter and Doc Hart were the trumpets. James Porter was one of the first big-name trumpet players around Los Angeles. He was originally from Chicago but came to Los Angeles through San Francisco and Oakland in the early 20s. He was not a hot player but could play the blues and pretty things on his trumpet, usually playing a muted horn. He was well thought of and they used to call him the "King Porter of the Pacific Coast." He was a short, very dark man and was one of the cleanest, nicest dressed men I have ever known. He always looked like he had just stepped out of a tub of hot water. He was completely immaculate. He never drove an auto in his life, so I was sort of his built-in chauffeur. I always had a car so I used to pick him up and take him everyplace that we ever played together and then take him home afterwards.

Doc Hart, the other trumpet, came into the Mosby orchestra right after he was discharged from the army. After World War I was over, he had enlisted in the army when there was no war on. He served in the cavalry units in places like Fort Huachuca, Arizona. During that time, he had to play while riding a horse and had developed enormous range on his trumpet. He was a very strong player, right up to par on his horn.

Doc was his nickname, and I never heard him called by any other. He was one of the playboys around town, tall, six feet two or so, a very light complected man and most women considered him to be very attractive. He was going with a sporting girl over in San Bernardino, about 80 miles away from Los Angeles, and used to commute back and forth. On one trip, he was involved in an automobile accident and was killed.

Baby Lewis was the drummer, a very, very good drummer and the first person I ever saw who played a vibraharp or bells. He was also an excellent trumpet player. Many times he'd be sitting at his drums, thumping with one hand and with a trumpet in the other, doing an excellent job playing both at the same time. When John Hammond first came out to the West Coast, Baby Lewis was one of Hammond's favorites but nothing ever jelled with him.

Baby Lewis was a very well educated man, but he did a whole lot of wrong things. For instance, back in the 'twenties, he was a member of the Sonny Clay band when this was one of the first groups from Los Angeles to go to Australia. While he was there, Baby committed so many wrong deeds like getting drunk, being rowdy and coming close to taking sexual pleasures from certain ladies, that he was practically deported.

I'll always remember something that happened when we were with the Mosby band. I was only seventeen then but Baby was already married and had a couple of children. He went to work one night but didn't get home until about ten o'clock the next morning. His wife wanted to know why he was so late and where had he been. He told her he had started home from work the previous night and had run into a bear. The bear ran him up a tree and he wasn't able to come down until ten o'clock the next morning.

Now this may not sound too ridiculous to people who don't know Los Angeles, but let me explain. I never heard about bears being anywhere nearby and besides, what would one be doing on the streets of Los Angeles, which at that time was about the fifth biggest city in the United States?

An ex-army man named Ed Perkins, whom we all called Perk, played tuba with Mosby since string bass wasn't yet popular. Walter Johnson was the pianist in Curtis Mosby's band in the late 'twenties and early 'thirties. He was an older musician, originally from Boston, Massachusetts and had gone to Boston Conservatory of Music. Needless to say, he was an excellent, well-versed musician, a good pianist, a good writer, and arranged music very well. In our early days with the Mosby Blue Blowers, he rehearsed the new shows that came in and was a very valuable man in the band.

In the late 'twenties and early 'thirties, the Apex was the biggest night club on the east side of Los Angeles, the ghetto area.

Like the Cotton Club in New York, the clientele was about 95% white. The rich people, actors in silent movies and those who knew what was going on in show biz went slumming first class at the ultra modern, elite Apex Club. We worked there for about a year. Later on, this same club changed its name and became famous as the Alabam.

Toward the end of high school, a few weeks before graduation, Mosby started the second unit of his Apex night club. This was at Grant and Bush near Chinatown, in San Francisco. It was the first black-oriented night club in San Francisco and featured black artists and musicians. I went north with the group and played at the opening. It was very successful for a time but when it fizzled out, we came back to Los Angeles.

While I was playing up north, I had missed my high school graduation and the chance to walk across the stage to get my diploma. I hadn't minded missing the big occasion but my mother had been disappointed about my not having been in the graduation ceremony. So she was pleased when, after I returned home, the high school president handed the diploma to me personally.

During the time I was working at the Apex night club in Los Angeles, Duke Ellington came to town and from then on, our paths crossed many times. He had come west to make his first picture, *Check and Double Check*. The Hollywood studio people were so involved in what they were doing and unfamiliar with music that they didn't think Ellington could be considered a big band without strings. The big moguls out at the studio said to Duke, "We can't understand how you are going to have a big orchestra in this extravaganza when you don't even have any violins," which shows you how square these people at the studios were about jazz. They told Duke he'd have to get some strings. So he needed to add them, but in 1930 there were no black viola or cello players working in the city and very few working anywhere else, for that matter. The best Duke could do was hire a few violin players.

As it happens, Ellington was staying in the best hotel for blacks in town, the Dunbar, which was next door to the Apex club.

Construction on this hotel began in 1926 and when it first opened, it was originally called the Summerville. But its name was changed soon after and it became the Dunbar. At any rate, Duke came into the club and saw me playing in the saxophone section. Then, when we did the waltzes, the other two saxes and I picked up our violins. At that time, it was fashionable to have violins playing waltzes and the pretty things. All three of us doubled violin in trio form, and when Duke heard us, he immediately hired us to come out and work with his band on *Check and Double Check*.

We didn't do very much but we did augment the original Ellington band, which consisted then of three saxophones, Johnny Hodges, Harry Carney and Barney Bigard; three trumpets, Artie Whetsel, Cootie Williams and Freddy Jenkins; two trombones, Juan Tizol and "Tricky Sam" Nanton, Wellman Braud on bass, Sonny Greer on drums, Freddy Guy on guitar and Duke on piano. I don't remember whether we were actually shown in the picture or heard on the sound track. We may even have been left on the cutting-room floors for all I know, but we worked together on that movie.

Duke came back in February 1934, and I remember he called me up and said, "I need you." He had added Otto Hardwick as an alto player but, shortly after the band arrived in Los Angeles, Otto disappeared for two or three weeks. No one knew where he was. Chances are he found a lady friend, stayed drunk and had a big time. While he was out, I worked with the band as lead saxophone. The band had several engagements and I recall playing a few dates with them at the Sweets chain of ballrooms in California, one in Fresno, another in Oakland and I think there were another couple, besides. Ellington always got good turn-outs.

Around that same time, Duke made *Murder at the Vanities*. I played *Ebony Rhapsody*, and I am on the sound track of that movie. Then the Ellington band did a picture with Mae West called *It Ain't No Sin*, and I worked with Duke again. This picture was released as *Belle of the Nineties*. In one of the jazz books there is a picture showing me with the Ellington group taken at that time. I saw this photo recently and it suddenly hit me with a shock to realize that everyone in it was dead except me!

Over this period of time, I got to know Duke as a friend. About 1933, he invited me to join him permanently as an addition, not a replacement. I couldn't accept because at that time my father had had a stroke and the role of father of the family had become mine. Even though Duke was persuasive, I stuck with it and told him I couldn't go.

Ellington had so many different facets such as his arrangements, his compositions, and the manner in which he featured his men and himself as a person. He was loaded with a sensational brand of showbiz b.s. and used it to good advantage. For years, he would come and throw his arm around me, hug me and say "Marshal, when are you going to come into my orchestra and make it sound good?" which was a typical Ellington b.s. line. At the same time, he'd be rubbing his cheek against mine and he always needed a shave. He'd keep rubbing my face until it felt like I had been scraped by sandpaper. I'd answer "Well, Duke, when you decide to turn your pockets inside out and give me a nice big salary, then I will consider it!" Conversation over.

In the early 50s, Ellington's band was booked into Las Vegas. Johnny Hodges, his star alto player, was about to leave him to start his own small group with Lawrence Brown, Sonny Greer, and a few others. A seven piece group, I think. Duke needed an alto player to take Johnny's seat and he knew I was laying out on the coast as I had been for the previous few years. He thought all he had to do was ask me. Actually, I might have joined Duke at that time if he had just called a little sooner. But it so happened that I was already in the East with Basie, who had asked me only two weeks earlier! So I never was a regular member of the Ellington orchestra. By the way, Duke hired Willie Smith, a great alto player, to replace Hodges, instead.

The last time I actually played with the Ellington band, both Ellington and Basie were booked to play a series of two band dates together in the New England states. This was in the mid-sixties or so. Ellington's lead alto player was, I believe, Hilton Jefferson. Either he was ill or there was illness in his family.

Whichever, Hilton couldn't make the appearance. Instead, I played lead with both bands! I'd play with Basie, get off the stand at the end of our set, then go over and play with the Ellington band for their set.

I played again with Ellington in the early 'seventies, for the very last time, but this was not with the complete band. My brother Ernie was also in this extravaganza done for television and I recall Harry Carney being there and just a few other members of the band.

Among Duke's talents are the fact that he had wonderful recall of any music he ever heard. I was not the only person he listened to and liked while he was in Los Angeles during the early 'thirties. As I mentioned, there were three saxophonists who doubled violin at the Apex and all three of us were hired for a movie. Another person appearing at the Apex was a gal who sang and danced in the floor show. She also caught Duke's fancy. That was Ivie Anderson, and he hired her as his band vocalist. Besides, Duke first heard trombonist Lawrence Brown when we were both in the Mosby group. A few years later, when Duke had decided to add a third trombone to his band, he remembered hearing Lawrence. He sent his agent, Irving Mills, out to hear him playing with Les Hite at the Cotton Club. Irving Mills liked him fine and Lawrence was invited to join the Ellington band.

3
Around Los Angeles

Out in Culver City on Washington Boulevard, near the MGM studio, there was a huge place called Frank Sebastian's Cotton Club. This was one of the largest clubs in the United States at that time. To give you an idea, on Saturday nights when it was full, they could serve formal meals to about a thousand people. They put on three shows a night with a chorus line, a headline entertainer, a comedian and so on. When the top names in the entertainment business came to Los Angeles, they were featured either at the Cotton Club or the Coconut Grove. Those were *the* places in Los Angeles in those days.

While I was still in high school, the house band at Sebastian's was led by Leon Herriford. He was maybe fifteen years older than me, which, in my estimation, made him an older guy. He was another saxophone player, a handsome man with quite a bit of Indian blood who looked more Indian than black, with straight hair and all. He died long ago at an early age, probably in his late 40s or so.

Back in the middle 1920s, he and some of his musicians used to come to our house early in the morning, between three and four o'clock, after they got off work. They'd wake my father up and beg him to let me come to work for them. Of course my father told them "No," as I was still in school. Besides, I was already working from eight at night until one in the morning, playing dance music, and, incidentally, was still managing to get to my Spanish class at five minutes to eight every morning!

Leon Herriford did persuade Lawrence Brown to leave the Curtis Mosby job and go to work with his band at the Cotton Club. Sebastian's Cotton Club was an important place to play. It was a first-class club where you'd hear and meet some of the finest artists and personalities in the world. More important, a band might stay there for years, so it was a steady job. Shortly after Lawrence began working there, Louis Armstrong was the starring artist at the Cotton Club. While Louis was in Los Angeles, he cut some of his early phonograph records fronting the Herriford group. Lawrence was in that band and can be heard on those records. This was the time, also, when Louis had the misfortune of being busted.

About that same time, Sebastian hired Les Hite to replace Herriford and that's when I came in. Actually, there was a short transition period between Herriford and Hite when McKinney's Cotton Pickers worked at Sebastian's. McKinney's had the typical instrumentation of bigger bands at that time, which was five brass and four rhythm. But the saxophone section, headed by Don Redman, had four men. When Les Hite's band was booked to play there, it was decided that Les ought to have four saxes, too. I was the person he hired to be the fourth sax.

So now I was to play at the famous Cotton Club. Les Hite, my new boss, was an ordinary looking man, not a beauty, but not a bad looking fellow, either. He was a very good dresser and he had a great personality, which made him attractive. He was not a flamboyant leader like Cab Calloway or Ellington but he had his ways and he was as well thought of in Los Angeles as they were in the East.

I was playing with Lawrence Brown again but that only lasted for a couple of years. As I said, Duke Ellington had heard Lawrence Brown play when we were with Mosby at the Apex. In 1932, he sent Irving Mills, his agent, out to the Cotton Club. They invited Lawrence to be a member of the Ellington orchestra and go on the road with them. It was because of a car that Lawrence decided to leave Les and join Duke!

Lawrence was a strange duck about his cars. When he bought a new auto, he'd wash it completely in and out before he took it out on the street. And when he brought it back in the evening, he'd completely wipe off the entire auto again. And every time he drove his car, it had to be washed before it was put away. Lawrence's pride and joy at that time was a beautiful sixteen cylinder Cadillac he'd just bought himself. He had to pay for it some way, so when Duke offered him about fifteen dollars more a week than he was getting, he joined the Ellington band.

I, too, was interested in cars from the time I was a teenager,

26

but in a little different way. I had learned to drive using a stick shift, but on a Federal truck, not on a car. The way that happened is that a junk dealer lived a couple of doors down the street from us and he owned the truck. His son took me out and gave me instructions, so I learned how to drive on that truck.

Of course I wanted a car of my own. I was about fourteen when I got my first one, a model T Ford. I bought that car. That is to say my father actually bought it for me, with money saved up from winning the amateur contests and other work I had done. I really wasn't licensed to drive by myself. In those days they gave a license to a fourteen year old child if he could pass the test and an adult was in the car with him. I got my first license in 1926 when I was fourteen and a permanent one in 1928. By then, I had been working regularly and had enough money to buy a nice car for the family, too. It was a 1928 Buick sedan, what we used to call a "family car." At the same time, I had my little raggedy Model T Ford.

I was what was called in those days "a hot rodder." Sometimes I had two or three model T Ford four cylinder automobiles as they only cost about $35 to $50 apiece and I was making that much with amateur contests and other little jobs I did. Even though I was just a kid, I was fortunate enough to be working pretty steadily so I always had a little money of my own.

What we did, when I was fifteen or sixteen years old, was to upgrade Model T's for speed. You could build up one of these autos into a racing car. The original Fords had only a foot shift without a hand gear. That would be one of the first things we'd take out and replace with a Chevrolet manual transmission. We'd call it a 3-1 ratio for gears. I didn't do all the work myself but I did a lot of it and for years always had grease under my fingernails.

On Sundays when we had the time, some of the other hot rodders and I would drive out to Muroc Dry Lake and race there on the part of the lake which is now Edwards Air Force base. This is the famous landing field now being used by the space shuttle. But in those days, dry lakes were for Sunday auto races. Some of the mechanics from the Miller Company, who modified cars for the Indianapolis races, were in our area over in Burbank and East

Los Angeles. We'd get together with them, have our motors ground, sanded, and built into larger dimensions for higher horsepower. These cars were not what you'd call beautiful. We'd cut them down strictly for speed. You wouldn't take your best girl friend out for a ride in that kind of an ugly car, a racer. If we wanted good looking cars, we'd get into a Chrysler convertible, which was new then. Then later, we all admired Auburns and in the mid-30's we had the first beautiful front wheel drive speed wagon, the Auburn Cord. It was a beautiful auto but drove like a truck. It was a fad at that time, a big thing, to go out and rent a good car for Sunday or a holiday. My favorite for taking out my girl friends in those days was a rented Chrysler convertible.

I always had girl friends from the time I was a little boy, but my first girl friend after I became a young man was Gladys Henderson, a chorus girl at Sebastian's. I met her originally while she was in her last year of high school. She was a year older than I, going to Manual Arts High, while I was at Jefferson High School. We met at still another school, Polytechnic High, while taking a summer school class. Gladys was the first girl I really started going steady with. We went around together for three or four years. She wanted to get married but I couldn't consider it because, by then, I had my family to take care of. Instead, Gladys wound up marrying a friend of mine, Buck Clayton. I'm sure it was because she liked Buck, who was talented and also a very good-looking fellow, but another motive could have been that he was booked for a tour to China and she wanted to go along.

This is the background on that. Earl Dancer, a New York show producer, was married to Ethel Waters. I don't know how good a show producer he was, as the one he did on Broadway lasted about five minutes, I heard. Earl Dancer was not a musician either, but when he came out to Los Angeles, he formed an orchestra which he had Buck Clayton lead for him.

Buck got an offer to go to China through a fellow named Teddy Weatherford who had been there for many years and had been sent home to the States to get an orchestra to take back and work in Shanghai.

The orchestra that he actually came for was Les Hite's but

28

we wouldn't accept the job because it didn't pay enough money for us. They only offered to pay the musicians the equivalent of about $50 a week away from home in Shanghai and we were already making much more than that. We had a starting salary of $55 a week, living and eating at home. Besides, once every month or two, we were getting a picture job in Hollywood. It wasn't steady but we were averaging about $100 a week and that was good money in the early 30's.

Up until then, I never knew Buck Clayton very well. We never worked a job together that I can remember and we never really hung out together, either. The fact is, in those days you were sort of a big shot if you worked at Sebastian's and the other guys looked up to you as having the best job in town and working in the best band, which was true. When I was working at Sebastian's, I was one of the big shots. We didn't go out to get to know the other fellows; they came out and tried to know us. So one way and another, I didn't get to know Buck although he was pretty good friends with some of the fellows I knew like Bumps Myers and Eddie Beal.

Originally, I think Buck knew something about piano. Then all of a sudden I looked up and saw him working and jobbing around town with the Charlie Echols' orchestra playing trumpet. I heard him playing high notes on his trumpet when it was a rarity to be able to control the notes at high range. Buck had very good chops. After I heard him play, I tried to get him into the Les Hite orchestra but it was about that time that Weatherford hired Earl Dancer's group to go to Shanghai, with Buck as leader. The way things go in show business is that the person who gets the job gets to be called band leader of the group. Buck had this chance so it became his group, his first orchestra, and he went on tour with it. And with my girl friend.

After Gladys, I had a lot of girls. There used to be a place, the 42nd Street drugstore, where the young guys hung out in the daytime. It was where most of the girls from the Golden State Insurance Company came to have lunch. This insurance company was black-owned and located at that time in between 42nd and 41st Streets on Central Avenue, one block from the Alabam. The company had a habit of hiring nothing but pretty girls, which was one of the prime requisites I believe. You could go upstairs and find the secretaries and book keepers and all the girls working there were the prettiest ones who had graduated from Jefferson, Polytechnic, or Manual Arts, the three main high schools at that time. The fellow who started the company also started out contributing pretty girls, because he had three gorgeous daughters and all three of them worked for the company.

Around lunch time for an hour or two you'd find the beautiful flowers of the city who were working at Golden State Insurance at the 42nd Street drugstore. All the sharpies around town who knew how to meet girls would congregate there. These pretty girls drew customers. Some of the fellows who hung out were the college boys. But lots of us had gone to work right after high school graduation and we had to compete with these college boys, the Alphas, the Kappas, the Omegas and what have you. I was one of the fellows who hung out to meet the girls. There weren't too many other musicians there because most of us worked until two, three, or four in the morning and they were still sleeping at noon. But I was on the street to meet the pretty girls there.

There were a few other fellows I knew around the drug store, too. My friend Marvin Johnson married Eola, a beautiful secretary who worked at Golden State Insurance Company. About that time, Red Callender came into town and also used to be in the vicinity. I think he had already been married by then to a girl out of Seattle who we called Big Margie. There were two girls who were called Big Margie and Little Margie who I first worked with in San Francisco. Red went with Big Margie and I was under the impression that he had married her. But at that particular time he was single, before he married Emma Priestly.

Working in a place like Sebastian's, there were many, many girls to be had, in the chorus line and in the customer line. It didn't really matter that much. It was a lot of fun; everybody had a lot of fun in those days. My mother liked all the girls I brought home. She was a very sweet lady and it often seemed to me that the girls liked my mother as much or better than they liked me! I played around like most young men do and I never stopped fooling around until I married my wife.

By then in the early 30s, my parents weren't working any more as a group but they still gave music lessons. My mother taught piano, rehearsed singers, worked with anyone doing a concert, or if they needed to learn a tune, she'd teach it to them, so she stayed busy. In those days before polyester, I used a whole lot of white shirts for work. I used to wear one or two every night and my mother always did them up. She'd wash and iron them for me. When I got to the place that I started making good money, I came to her one day and said, "Mother, you don't need to ever do another shirt for me in your life." I didn't want her working so hard and ironing them anymore.

When I first went out to play with Les Hite at the Cotton Club, Lionel Hampton was the drummer with the band. A few musicians who had been with Herriford stayed on at Sebastian's and now worked for Les Hite. They were the "crossovers." However, I first heard Hamp a few years before that, when he was with Paul Howard's Quality Serenaders playing a dance hall located at 54th and Central. In the late 20s, there were Saturday afternoon dances. All the kids went, including me, because in those days I liked to dance. However, I didn't get to know Lionel until we were both working for Les Hite. He was enough older than me that we didn't socialize.

George Orendorff, who knew Lionel from Chicago, had been in many of the same groups. He was the trumpet player with the old Paul Howard Quality Serenaders. Then he had also worked with Leon Herriford and sort of moved into Les Hite's band when it was the one booked at the Cotton Club, so he was another cross-over musician. He was a light complected man, an excellent trumpet player, very loyal, a distinguished type of gentleman. He played the instrument correctly and could do a lot of Louis Armstrong type of music. That was because he'd come up from Chicago at the time Louis and King Oliver were there. Later, after Les broke up his big band, George quit playing, went into the postal service and worked there until retirement. He lived a good life and died only recently.

31

George was one of the people who suggested to Reb Spikes that he should hire Lionel Hampton when Hamp came to Los Angeles from Chicago. I'm not clear on whether George was instrumental in having Lionel come out here or just suggested that he be hired after he was already here. But it was George, along with Les Hite, who sent Lionel in to Reb Spikes. Incidentally, Gladys Hampton, Lionel's wife, and George's wife, Velma, were two of the best seamstresses in town. They worked together for many years, doing sewing for the Hollywood stars.

There were two Spikes brothers, Reb and Johnny, who together started the first music store for blacks in Los Angeles at 12th and Central. Reb Spikes was an older man, probably older than my father, and he had the luxury of having people come to him with musical engagements. His clientele included most of the musicians around town so he used to put bands together but I don't ever recall that Reb, himself, played any instrument. Later, he became a big real estate operator and earned a good living from that.

But, back in its heyday, Reb Spikes' store sold musical instruments, reeds, sheet music, and so on. In those days, people bought a lot of sheet music and a few records, too. Everyone at that time had a wind-up phonograph but there weren't that many people recording, or records to buy. Most of the bands making records were like Paul Whiteman and Abe Lyman and that type of music. There were few records for the black clientele and these were on Okeh, Vocalion, and the other minor labels. There was also a pretty big demand for piano rolls because a lot of people had player pianos.

Jelly Roll Morton was one of the musicians who brought many nice things into vogue with his player piano rolls. I met him for the first time at Reb Spikes's place when he happened to be in Los Angeles. He knew my father and Dad took me over to meet him. Jelly Roll was quite a pompous type of fellow, almost arrogant in his manners, but you had to respect him for what he had accomplished.

My dad introduced me and Morton said to me, "Hello, young Royal, how are you?" At that time there was a lot of

32

confusion about what to call me because my father and I were both named Marshal.

I answered, "Just fine."

Then he asked me, "Are you playing the piano?"

I said, "No. Piano players should be women because my mother plays piano. I think it's a woman's instrument, so I wouldn't play the piano."

I added that I thought only sissies played piano. That hurt Jelly Roll's feelings and throughout the years, he never forgot me and what I said. He never liked me. I met him again in later years when he came back to Los Angeles and was staying with some friends of mine. He said hello, he remembered me alright, but I don't think he ever really forgave me.

It was about this same time that Lionel was becoming famous around town as a great drummer. He was an excellent rhythm player, kept good time and could do drum solos. Before joining Les, he had also been with Herriford but the rumor was that he was not paid by either leader but was directly on Sebastian's payroll, making $75 a week.

As Lionel got into his exhibitionist phase, he emulated a sensational drummer he had seen playing at Grauman's Chinese Theater. The movie playing there was called *Trader Horn* and, as was customary at that time, there was also a stage show. One of the acts in the show was a group called the Norman Thomas Quintet. There were two sons, very handsome boys, who were both dancers. But the important person in the groups was the flashiest drummer I have ever seen and, as a matter of fact, that anybody else had ever seen at that time. His name was Rastus Crump. He was all exhibition and he could do miraculous things with his drum sticks. He'd throw them around, hold them under his nose or under his arms as part of the prologue. For his finale, he'd grab the curtains as they were pulling them up and down, hanging on to the bottom as they went thirty feet, forty feet up in the air. Sometimes the curtains went up and down several times for encores and he'd be hanging on all the while.

Lionel used Rastus Crump as a role model as he got into his exhibitionist stage. Just as Rastus Crump had done, Lionel used to go around beating on tables, on the glasses filled with drinks and such as part of his act. He went so far as to copy this man's style of going off stage and then sliding back on, hitting a cymbal while lying flat on the sort of large tray that the bus boys used for clearing tables. Lionel adopted this as his finale when he did his drum solos.

Hamp was always trying to enlarge his presence in the band and get himself recognized as a star in his own right. It got to be that he was almost his own boss in the Les Hite band, as he gathered prestige. During this time, he made some recordings with either the Leon Herriford band or the Les Hite band, or maybe it was with both. I'm not sure which. They did some things including *Song of the Islands* on which Lionel first recorded as a vibraharp player.

Lionel had learned how to finger the vibraharp by using a little bell set belonging to Harvey Brooks, one of the two piano players at Sebastian's. At that time, Lionel couldn't afford a whole set of vibraphones so Harvey loaned him those little bells.

After work, Lionel would go jamming practically every night at the after hour joints we all frequented. He just loved to play. He would sometimes drive piano players crazy by sitting down with them and having them play what we called comp, that is playing just the chords. Meanwhile, Lionel would be playing two-finger piano in the upper register. Whatever anyone would play, he would try to mimic later on his vibraharps. Anytime he had a chance, he'd sit down and get the pianist to play chords while he practiced his one-finger improvising.

Sometimes he would wear out two or three piano players during the course of a night. He'd drink and play his two finger piano until day break. There were nights that he drank too much and got so drunk that I had to drive him home in my car. I'd ring the door bell to his place and just dump him on the front porch for his wife or his mother-in-law to bring him in.

Lionel left Les Hite in 1934 to form his first big band. I could have gone with him but I remained with Les at the Cotton Club. Hamp hired some good musicians for that band, some of the best musicians who were on the coast at that time. Let me add here

34

that although these fellows were living on the West Coast, nobody, hardly ever, *came* from the coast. Most of the so-called "West Coast musicians" were people who had migrated west from Kansas City, Dallas, New Orleans, and so on. There were very, very few local musicians.

Hampton's band had two great tenor saxes, Herschel Evans and Don Byas, who were two of the finest tenor players in the country at that time. Also, he had Teddy Buckner on trumpet. This Teddy Buckner was no relation to the alto saxophone player Teddy Buckner with Jimmie Lunceford. The Los Angeles Teddy was an only child. His family had come to California from Texas when he was small and I had known him for some time. We attended junior high school together. Teddy was a first rate man, was employed in many movies as a look-alike, sound-alike for Louis Armstrong.

Sometime in the 'forties, Teddy organized a Dixieland type band. His group has played for about one hundred years, or for such a long time it seems like that, at Disneyland, on one of those riverboats. The last time I saw him he was fine and still blowing, although he had become quite heavy.

Lionel got his big band booked up the Pacific Coast, but even with all these good players, the band wasn't that successful, so he came back into Los Angeles and formed a smaller group. I'm not sure just how large, about seven pieces or so. They worked in a place called the Paradise Club on Main Street, which was one of the better night clubs at that particular time. In 1937, Benny Goodman discovered him there and invited him to come with his band to augment the trio of Goodman, Teddy Wilson and Gene Krupa, making it a quartet. From there, Lionel became very successful and world renowned.

4
The Cotton Club

Without a doubt, Les Hite's band was the best band on the Pacific Coast at that time. In those days, everybody said you had to go to New York to get your "stamp." But Les had gotten his stamp out West. He had a very good musical band, with some very fine musicians in it, although the music may not have included all of the nuances of jazz. In the band when I began with Les were Lionel as drummer and Lawrence Brown, who had joined him when Herriford lost the job at the Cotton Club.

Sebastian's Cotton Club was a terrific place. Everything was first class. They had anything you wanted to eat: steaks, chops, chicken or sandwiches. There was a Filipino fellow who made sandwiches and I recall a giant soup tureen, filled fresh each day with about five gallons of soup. There were three dance floors; the big one in the center was where customers danced and which was also used for the floor show presentation. The two on the sides were only in use when the place was at full capacity and for special occasions.

In the kitchen at Sebastian's, there were two or three long tables that would each seat about twelve people, with a bench on either side. Sebastian fed all of his help, the kitchen people, chef, waiters, show girls, band and everybody that worked for him. About midnight was eating time. After we had done a show and played a dance set, we would take about a 45 minute break to eat. Meanwhile, out front, there'd be two piano players on the floor with small movable pianos. Next to each there'd be one or two girl singers and they went from table to table, taking requests while we were eating.

The menu would change every night, all the seven nights a week that everyone worked. One night maybe it would be steak, another chicken or stew. These were well planned meals each and every night. They always had the huge tureen of soup, which you could have as much of as you wanted and the soup alone was enough to fill you up. Each night, it was a different type of soup, always fresh made. You could bet that Friday was clam chowder and it was always terrific. In fact, the food there was some of the best that I have ever eaten over a long period of time. And I ate a midnight meal at Sebastian's for nearly eight years.

There were three full shows a night and the last one went on at two in the morning. Frank Sebastian always had the best attractions in the country that he could hire. When I began there, the featured artist was Louis Armstrong, who fronted the Les Hite band. Previously, he had fronted the Leon Herriford band at the time he was unceremoniously busted for having one measly marijuana cigarette in his hand.

The star of the show that followed after him was Fats Waller, who was there for quite a time. The big acts interacted with the band in different ways. When Fats Waller was there, maybe a month or so at a time, the band accompanied him on practically every number. He also had arrangements which featured various parts of the band. The smaller groups would be a trumpet, me on clarinet and a few others. He'd sing and play, do his comical things. Fats was a great performer and he fronted Les Hite's band just as though it was his own.

Fats was a very likeable man: a big man and a big drinker. In those days, it was mostly hard liquor. His favorite was Old Overholt, a Canadian whisky, but he also drank champagne. He liked to keep a supply of these two beverages on hand in his dressing room

When he went to buy his liquor, he went to the place where we all hung out after hours. It was called the 54th Street Drug Store, located on the corner of 54th and Central Avenue. They served food, and if you were the right person, you could buy whisky by the bottle after hours. Fats was new in town, he never stayed in a hotel but roomed with a private family, so he didn't have any credit locally even though he was a very well paid performer. When he went to the all-night drug store and tried to buy some champagne and his Old Overholt on credit until pay day, they turned him down.

Fats and I had gotten to be friends, and I did a very dangerous thing. I was pretty well known at the drug store so I told the fellow to give Fats what he wanted and that I would stand for his bill. Fats would buy $50-70 dollars worth of liquor at a time, which was a whole lot of liquor in those days. And he bought only the best: Mumm's champagne was his choice and it was even more popular than the other brands then. It was quite a chance that I took and if I'd had to pay, it would have been a disaster. But Fats was true to his word, he never owed me one dime and I didn't have to make good for his bill.

In the Les Hite band's saxophone section, I was on lead. My two old friends from Leon Rene's band were also in the section. Marvin Johnson, my look-alike friend, played second alto and Charlie Jones was on tenor. Les Hite also played alto for a time. Later, Bumps Myers was a second tenor saxophone. This is how Bumps came to be with the band.

About the mid-30's, the Les Hite band played a date in Bakersfield, which was about 125 miles away. Coming back to Los Angeles from the engagement, Les Hite had an automobile accident. He hadn't driven very far, it was just before he got to the Grapevine, when he met another automobile head on. Joe Bailey, the bass player, had had a considerable amount to drink. He was in the back seat and didn't get a scratch. But Les had all his front teeth knocked out, and cut his lip so badly that we didn't know if he could play his saxophone anymore. The rest of the fellows came back into Los Angeles and nobody knew what was going to happen. There was Les in a hospital in Bakersfield, we were all in Los Angeles and we had engagements lined up to play. The guys got together and decided that I should lead the band. We went out on the road to take care of all of our bookings and I fronted the group. To restore the saxophone section back to four men, I hired Bumps Myers to play until at least we found out if Les was going to be able to come back and play. But when he was released from the hospital, it turned out that Les couldn't play, so that is how Bumps got to be a regular.

Bumps Myers was a couple of years older than me and was also from Los Angeles. We first met at Lorenzo Flennoy's when I was a young teenager. Lorenzo was a childhood friend and we had known each other from the time we were about five or six years old. He and his brother Otis lived across the fence from me on an adjoining street. We were always close, almost like brothers. Four of us kids had a tin pan band when we were little: Lorenzo, Otis, Jack McVea (who wrote *Open the Door Richard*) and I. For instance, we'd make a bass violin out of a wash tub with a string and a stick, and we used to play with things we picked up around the house like washboards, frying pans, and cooking pots, no real instruments. My violin was far too elite for this group. We played, sang in harmony and so on and we had a lot of fun with it. It was at that time that Lorenzo started wanting to be a band leader and he never changed his mind.

As we grew older, he kept sort of an open house. Lorenzo had been studying the piano from the time he was quite young and Otis turned out to be a very good drummer. Because there was a piano at his place, the fellows liked to congregate there. Lorenzo used to invite younger musicians over for little parties which were to come eat and drink, bring your horn and play. Bumps was one of the fellows who hung out there, who'd come by with his saxophone and blow. He had a nice, natural talent but not too much formal training. After Bumps joined Les, we always went back and forth to work together.

Lorenzo got his bands together from these young musicians who turned up and jammed at his house. He incorporated Red Callender and a lot of the other guys around town into his bands. These were always a bunch of young fellows coming up, eager to play and who didn't expect much in the way of pay. If they got four, five, or six dollars a night for playing, that would be a good salary for them since their fathers were most likely supporting the whole family on about twenty dollars a week. Now and then, if he had an engagement over the week-end, I'd play with his group for the kind of little dances they'd work, like for a girls club or the YWCA. During the years I was working with Les Hite, Lorenzo Flennoy usually had the big band at the Alabam, with his customary bunch of young musicians.

Our trumpet section had a very good lead player in George Orendorff who had been with the Quality Serenaders, with Herriford and was another cross-over into the Les Hite band. The second player was James Porter, whom I mentioned playing with when we were both with Mosby.

The third trumpet player was Lloyd Reese, who originally started out as an alto player but he came into the Les Hite band on trumpet. Lloyd was the best trumpet player to come out of the West Coast during the 30s, in my opinion. During the time when he was going to Whittier College studying music, I got him to come down and meet Les. Lloyd was so poor in those days, he couldn't afford to buy oil for his car. He used to put water in the motor to keep it from burning up while he was driving to and from college and then to work at eight each night. He was one of the few real California musicians, and he grew up in the Venice area, near the ocean. Lloyd was later renowned as a music teacher, had his own studio and there were many famous players whom he taught various instruments: saxophone, piano, trombone and trumpet. Several among his many pupils became famous. Dexter Gordon is one that comes to mind.

There were two piano players around the Les Hite band. One or two were often needed to play shows and for intermissions. Most of the years, the pianists were Harvey Brooks and Lawrence Brown's brother, Harold, but earlier, for a time, there was Henry Prince. Our guitar player was Bill Perkins and the bass was a young man out of Seattle, Joe Bailey.

For many of the shows, original music would be written. Sometimes we bought stocks which we'd cut up and pull apart. From the time I first went to work at the Cotton Club, there was a team called Broomfield and Greeley who developed the shows. In those days, the Cotton Club had only black artists, and they'd change the show completely every two or four weeks. Leroy Broomfield and Aurora Greeley started out as a dance team and danced together for years and years. They looked enough alike to be brother and sister, both black and about 5'4" or 5'5". Leroy had lived in Los Angeles since 1927. As a pair, Broomfield and Greeley were the best show producers in town and produced the Cotton Club shows for many years. Aurora was a dance teacher, one of the best. They did everything, including the choreography. They had a line of about a dozen chorus girls and would have about four or five different routines. Leroy kept up with all of the latest New York musicals and what was new on the screen in the way of music and picked up on these to incorporate for the shows.

Then, they'd add to the regular cast with famous dance acts such as Eddie Rucker, out of New York, and Peg Leg Bates. When Louis Armstrong came to town to do a movie, he'd appear at Sebastian's and was considered to be part of a show. If Fats Waller was appearing, he would be incorporated into a show and so on. We had many wonderful acts working there. I remember that one of our comedians was Eddie Anderson, who sometimes worked with his brother and also did comedy with John Taylor. Taylor was one half of the dance act called Rutledge and Taylor. These fellows did a type of dancing which was popular at that time called "me and my shadow", which they had been doing since the late 20's. Later, Eddie Anderson was corralled by Jack Benny for his show where he performed for many years known as Rochester.

When Broomfield and Greeley developed a new show, we had to rehearse after we got off at three in the morning, and we'd rehearse until eight, nine or even ten in the morning for maybe two or three days. At one time, they were changing the shows every two weeks. It was a lot of overtime work and we did not get paid extra for any rehearsal time.

Getting back to the personnel in the Les Hite band, we had two trombones: when I first joined, Lawrence Brown was still in the band and the other one was Sonny Craven, who we called Mush Mouth because he played things with plungers in a similar order to "Tricky" Sam Nanton. He did the growl type solos and so on. Sonny Craven had been with Les for some time before I joined and stayed with Hite for the eight years I was with the band. He was a very quiet man, probably ten or twelve years older than I, and he never went out and jammed. He always used to say that when he got to the place where he could buy himself a brand new Cadillac and have himself his own home he'd be ready to die. Years later, it happened just like that. He bought himself a new Cadillac and a nice place to live, and, shortly afterwards, he died!

After Lawrence left to go with Duke, Les hired Parker Berry

to take his place. Well, nobody could replace Lawrence Brown, but there was an opening for a trombone player and Parker was hired. It was not mainly for his playing style but because he was a good arranger. From then on, although Les bought some outside charts, Parker did most of the arrangements for the band. He also started Buck Clayton arranging, sort of taught him the ins and outs, and Buck would probably give him credit for this.

My family chose him to look out for me when I first left town to go up north to San Francisco with Mosby when I was only seventeen. I stayed with him up there. He was an ordinary looking guy, but he had one unique habit. When he got up in the morning, the first thing he did was put his cap on. And he wore it throughout the rest of the day. He's the only person I ever knew to do that.

Peppy Prince was hired on drums in 1934 after Lionel left Les Hite. There were three musicians around town named Prince and they were all cousins. Peppy became the drummer with Les Hite, Wesley played bass with the original Nat "King" Cole Trio and Henry Prince played piano with Les for three, four or five years while we had other people for intermissions. Henry was originally from Chicago, the eldest of the three cousins. He played beautiful ballads and he took his style of playing from Earl Hines. At that time, Earl Hines was the master of the jazz piano and just about as good as you could find anywhere. Earl had played with Carroll Dickerson, Louis Armstrong and many other big stars. He was the one to copy until Art Tatum came on the scene, and then it was a different story. Art superseded everyone.

Peppy Prince was a very likeable man, nice looking and he had a great personality. Unlike Lionel, he did no tricks with the drums, no stick bouncing or anything like that. Even though he wasn't a great drummer, he sang well and added to his stature by singing all of the ballads as well as playing drums.

During those many years I was with the Les Hite band, it was practically a permanent fixture at Sebastian's Cotton Club. However, at various times, we would leave, maybe for four weeks at a time, to go on the road and work at various other places. In 1934, I recall that we went all the way up the Coast to

Seattle and Vancouver, Canada. It was the first time I had ever been that far from home.

While we were in Seattle, we heard an excellent young lady singer named Evelyn Williamson. She was working as a vocalist in a club owned by her brother-in-law, Noodles Smith. He was the big guy in the neighborhood who sort of ran things on his side of town. Since World War I, he owned two or three night clubs, gambling joints, wherever you made money. Evelyn was singing in one of his places and she was a first-rate ballad singer, as good as anybody around. Les liked her and later hired her to sing with his band. She was our band vocalist during the last couple of years that we worked Sebastian's.

Frank Sebastian, the owner of the Cotton Club, was tall, maybe six feet two. He was quite a handsome Italian man with a healthy looking shock of hair, always very immaculately dressed, and he had a welcoming, infectious smile. You could see him from quite a distance because he used to stand in the doorway with a light from the ceiling pointed downward to where he would stand. It would enhance his appearance and make him look as if he was practically on stage.

I know very little about Italian traditions, personally, but I was told from several different sources that Frank Sebastian followed an old custom about the way he kept clean. They said that he never actually bathed with soap and water. Instead, Sebastian had masseurs to come to the apartment he kept in the Cotton Club and rub him down with olive oil and other oils familiar to the Italian people. After that, they would take corn meal and rub all of the oil off him, taking away the impurities, the dirt and perspiration, cleansing him in that manner. Probably they'd shower him after after that. He always looked wonderful, immaculately dressed and groomed.

During his time there, he was closely acquainted with the people who ran the gambling ship *Rex*. This was a pleasure ship anchored far enough off shore so it was not subject to the California laws about gambling and drinking hours. Frank Sebastian had these people arrange for some gambling at Sebastian's. They installed it off to one side, concealed by the gold curtains and it was not known to the general public who patronized the place. Only a big time gambler or a notable was ever admitted.

The gambling room brought in a different type of clientele, people who spent money very readily, and was responsible for quite an influx of people into the club including a lot of the rich and famous. One of the people who came in quite often was Howard Hughes. He was a strange dude, not an extrovert in any manner. He sort of kept to himself, and never or very seldom had any money in his pocket. His business agent always traveled with him, had the money and paid all the bills.

At that time, one of the acts in the floor show was a comedian, a fellow called Dudley Dickerson. He was a big guy, weighed about 260 pounds and he toe danced in ballerina shoes! In that day or any other day, this act would be quite extraordinary. Howard Hughes would get money from his business agent and fill a saucer or plate on the table with a lot of silver dollars. They'd heat the coins up with the candle on the table until they were red hot. Then they'd throw the silver dollars on the floor at this huge man who was toe dancing. When Dudley picked up these heated coins, he'd immediately holler "Oh, that's a hot one!" This would make Hughes and some of the other people laugh and applaud.

The Les Hite Orchestra was probably the best dressed band that you would ever see. We had ten or twelve different changes of clothes and we were very proud of these uniforms, partly because we had bought them ourselves. We wanted to be sharp.

During those years, I saw a lot of the Hollywood people at the Cotton Club. One night, I was playing a solo out in front of the band and I saw a little fellow come near. He was doing a tango and was quite a terrific dancer. A lot of people had gathered around to watch him.

I was still out in front at the end of the tune. He came up to me and said, "I really admire the type of clothing that you fellows are wearing. Who does your tailoring?"

So I told him, "There's a place in the 6500 block on Hollywood Boulevard, called Macintosh, Hollywood Studio Tailoring." I added: "Just go out there and I'm sure the tailors will do a very good job for you."

He said "Thank you very much. I'm a new guy in town, just in this week. Texas Guinan sent for me. She thinks I'm the Rudolph Valentino type and wants me to do some acting out here. My name is George Raft."

Sure enough he went to Macintosh and apparently was very satisfied. They outfitted him and he became a regular customer there. After that, he always looked sharp. Speaking about this, I think it is the only time I can recall that I was in an organized group where I had to buy my own uniform. That is with the exception, of course, of owning a tuxedo. The union rules provide that each working musician must have one.

During the latter years that I was with Les Hite, the band was in a few movies. We were in *The Music Goes Round*, but we did not do the soundtrack for that one. During the early years of sound movies, the soundtrack was not necessarily made by the band seen on the screen. There were regular staff musicians who played those scores. I did *Murder in Swingtime* with Les Hite's band in 1937, at Paramount. I don't know whether the sound on that one was us or not. Even for the staff musicians, the money wasn't that big, only $125 a week. As for us, we were thrown the crumbs by allowing us to appear in the picture itself. This was called "side-line filming" and meant you were being shown on the screen but not heard.

Also in the mid-30's, there was a series of movies featuring the Marx Brothers. By chance, I was seen on the screen with the Les Hite band for *A Day at the Races* and I was also hired as a free lance musician at MGM by Georgie Stoll, the music director. So I played lead alto on the musical score for *A Day at the Races*, *A Day at the Circus*. as well as some of the other Marx Brothers movies and can be heard playing on those sound tracks.

Although the Cotton Club had an all-white clientele policy, there were several people who came in, what we used to call in those days "passing." We knew who they were. Also, a big star like Bill Robinson could come as a special guest. Naturally they would use him, have him come out on the floor and do a little dance during the show, but he was not an intermingling guest.

The only time I remember there being an Afro-American guest treated on a regular basis was when they had three world champions being honored there on the same night. Sitting at a regular table together that night were Max Baer, Carnero and Joe Louis, as guests.

As the 1930s continued, business was bad and stayed bad. Hard times fell on the Cotton Club just as they were also falling on all the other night clubs in the country. It was the Depression time. I think Hoover was president, talking about a chicken in every pot and nobody had a chicken nor a pot to put it in. The popularity of the Cotton Club started declining because there weren't enough people with money to come in and spend their money there. Sebastian tried all sorts of experiments. For the first time, he brought in white entertainment. He booked a white producer named Carol Norman, who was not a world-wide known entertainer, as you would expect, but he had a certain following. He was a lady, shall we say and brought in his own kind of crowd.

When Carol Norman was in charge, he tried to put on a New York type of show with all white performers but it was really not that successful. He brought along a small following, not as good as they had hoped for. Greenwich Village in New York was a long way from Culver City. One of the acts was the Frazee Sisters. These sisters sang duets and did a little bit of dancing. They were very good and had excellent arrangements. Jane Frazee's photo was on the sheet music of, I believe the song was, *Moon Glow*. Later, she married a cowboy Western movie star.

Sebastian hired all sorts of people to come in such as actors getting started in Hollywood, cowboys making Western films, and people like that. That didn't work out too well either, so he returned to his old format. He hired Valaida Snow from New York in 1935 to bring in a complete show and let the whole Broomfield and Greeley outfit go, excepting that Sebastian kept on certain of the noted performers.

Valaida brought almost an entire cast for the show with her. She had been a star in the show *Blackbirds of 1934*, and was a well-known personage at that time. She was a very attractive woman, she danced and was also an excellent singer. She was actually so good that Ethel Waters, who was a big star, had suggested to the producers and management that she be fired from an earlier edition of *Blackbirds*. I don't know if Valaida was actually let go at that particular time but there was a big discussion and a whole lot of hullabaloo about the situation. As I was only fourteen years old when all this happened, I don't know for sure, but the talk was that Ethel Waters had had her fired because Ethel couldn't follow her on the stage after she sang. Besides that, Valaida was one of the first lady trumpet players and she was an excellent player.

Valaida Snow really knew how to produce a show and she put on some of the best ones they ever had at Sebastian's. She featured the young man she was married to whose name was Ananias Berry, nicknamed Nyas. He worked with his brother James in an act called the Berry Brothers. For the finale, the youngest brother came in, too. Valaida also brought a whole line of girls with her and there was a lot of good, hard first-class tap-dancing from both the Berry Brothers and the chorus girls. Each one of the girls was capable of stepping out of the line and doing her own thing. Marie Bryant, who later was choreographer for many Hollywood films, was one of the chorines in her line along with another little girl who became my girl friend, Deanie Gordon. These girls were just sensational in their dancing. I recall that the dance craze called truckin' started at that time and those gals could really truck.

In 1935, about the same time that the Valaida Snow show came in, Les had to go out of town to Champaign when his mother passed. While he was away, I was elected to take over as leader of the band. I did all the rehearsals and the new show. Before that, I had helped to rehearse the band, but this was probably the first time I was in full charge of directing a band.

As far as the turn-out of customers was concerned, the Cotton Club just kept deteriorating. Frank was running into the red. About then, a big name at MCA, Ed Fishman, came along and tried to persuade Sebastian to put MCA attractions into the Cotton Club. Fishman was a big fat dude, one of MCA's main agents. In 1936 I think it was, he assured Frank Sebastian that if he'd allow MCA to put a band into the Cotton Club, in return they'd book the Les Hite band into the Texas Centennial Exposition in Dallas. That was a big lie and it didn't turn out at all. They put their MCA band into the Cotton Club all right but didn't book us anyplace, which left us out on a limb. That was my first experience with the MCA dynasty.

It was about this same time that Sebastian brought in a white band which might have been the one booked in by MCA. This was the Ben Pollack orchestra, playing music that was really just short of being Dixieland. For his engagement, Pollack sent to Galveston, Texas for a newcomer trumpet player to join his band. His name was Harry James. He was excellent and he enhanced the Pollack group. Shortly after, James met with real fame when he joined the Benny Goodman band.

When other bands would come in to the Cotton Club, we'd go out on the road doing one-nighters. We'd go up the coast through Oregon and Washington as far as Vancouver, Canada and also went east as far as Idaho and Montana. But we never played in the South. On one of these tours, I think it was in 1938, we were in Spokane, Washington, playing the big room of a club. There was a piano bar in the lobby and the pianist was pretty good, a young white fellow. He asked me what I thought about his playing and I advised him that he'd better get into a big city like Chicago, New York or Los Angeles if he wanted to further his career. Young Jimmy Rowles took my advice and turned up in Los Angeles the following year and became an important jazz pianist.

Also about that time, when we weren't working at the Cotton Club, we did various engagements around Los Angeles. There was a ballroom, the Zenda Ballroom, which for many years had featured white groups. Sometime around 1937-38, before the band disintegrated, I played there with Les Hite for Sunday afternoon dances. Later, the Zenda became a ballroom specializing in Latin music, with a Latin clientele. It is no longer in existence.

For eight years, except for our brief trips out of town, I worked at the Cotton Club seven nights a week, excepting when I had to lay off a night, but when they stopped having the big shows, Les Hite lost his job there in 1938.

Needless to say, the band was in disarray. We hadn't been working steady, now we were no longer at the the Cotton Club, so Les cut down the size of the band. We had two trumpets, Lloyd Reese and George Orendorff, Sonny Craven and Parker Berry on trombones, Marvin Johnson, Charlie Jones, Bumps Myers and myself on saxophones, Henry Prince on piano, Joe Bailey on bass and Peppy Prince on drums. We were hired to play a place in Hollywood which Frank Sebastian had taken over. It was called the Cubanola and featured Cuban entertainment. A pair of sensational Cuban dancers called Rene and Estelle, who had been playing in New York, had been sent for. The Conga line had just become very popular but the Cuban licks and rhythm were not too familiar to the fellows out west, particularly to our drummer. Peppy Prince could not get the beat one-two-three-*kick*, one-two-three-*kick*, the Conga line rhythm. He wasn't familiar at all with the lick, he wasn't too good a reader so we used to spend half the afternoon trying to teach him how to do it right. He never did get it and it ended up by our losing the job at the Cubanola.

Not long after that, Les decided to leave Los Angeles and take a band out on the road to New York. He worked one-nighters on into Chicago where his group eventually broke up due to union manipulations. They had two unions in Chicago, as in most cities: the white and the black unions. The south side (black union) made it hard for him because they tried to keep the Les Hite group from working in that town.

But Les wasn't really worried because he was subsidized by a multi-millionaire lady who saw to it that he lived happily ever after. He was very well taken care of, only drove Cadillacs, wore the best of clothes and had a pocket full of money for the rest of his life. She bought him a little ranch in Monrovia and property in Los Angeles, which he had until the day he died. Les Hite worked as this woman's pseudo-chauffeur, cap and all, but what really went on was another story altogether...

5
I Am The Father Of The Family

After I had been working at Sebastian's Cotton Club a couple of years, my Dad had a stroke. That was in late 1933. My uncle had gone East and was in New York at that time. It was now up to me to take over as the man of the house and I became "father" of the family. Dad died two years later in the fall of 1935. For several years, I provided for my mother, sister and helped raise my younger brother, Ernie. We all stayed on in the house.

Not too surprisingly, my brother Ernie also proved to have musical talent. At the urging of my uncle, he took up the trumpet when he was about seven or eight years old. Uncle Ernest took him in tow, repeating a pattern, because Uncle Ernie, too, had played trumpet along with the reeds at an early age. He tutored Ernie long enough to teach him how to read and get himself a decent embouchure.

After about a year, he decided it was time to put my brother in the hands of a real professional teacher. Arrangements were made with one of the better teachers in town, George Pacheco. At one time he had been among the leading players with the famous John Philip Sousa band. Pacheco had the use of a rehearsal room at the white union, Local 47 on Georgia Street, from which he taught. Ernie took lessons from him once a week from then on, over a number of years.

Pacheco retired and stopped teaching when Ernie was in his teens. However, by that time, Ernie did not need a teacher very much. He was quite advanced, had an impeccable embouchure and one of the main things George Pacheco taught him was breath control. Ernie learned how to blow and breathe from the lower part of the chest, which stood him in good stead in his future years.

After the lessons ended, my brother and I started experimenting with his embouchure and way of blowing. He started a sort of blowing where he could smile into his mouthpiece and then was able to blow another octave higher. This became one of the techniques used by some of the younger trumpet players coming up; what we generally term the "non-pressure system."

Ernie was influenced, of course, by several trumpet players. He liked Roy Eldridge and the cute things Rex Stewart did. When he was only fifteen, he learned to play *Boy Meets Horn,* the thing Rex wrote with half-valve notes, and he copied Rex so exactly you couldn't tell the two apart.

I can remember a time when I went out on the road with Les Hite. When I left, Ernie was two inches shorter than me but when I got back, just in a matter of a couple of months, I was two inches shorter than Ernie! He seemed to grow very fast and got to be six feet two and a half while I never grew to be more than five eight and a half. I'd talk about my little brother and here he was nearly a head taller than I was. Back in those days, Ernie was tall and I was the average height. But now it seems like the average for a young man is more like five ten or six feet and I'm considered to be a shorty.

Besides music, Ernie's other big interest was short-wave radio, which came about like this. Before he was even born, around 1920, radio was introduced. I was eight years old, still in grammar school and I became intrigued with this new invention. I started reading popular mechanics books and magazines which had instruction about how to make crystal radio sets. So I followed through. Before I left the school in the sixth grade, I was the first kid in my grammar school who actually made a usable radio. It was a crystal set. I'd take cereal boxes, wind them with different grades of wiring, put them out and then connect them to the crystal set. We didn't need any electric power to be connected to these crystal sets, nor batteries. They were truly wireless. It was the plainest form of what you'd call, these days, electronics.

My parents were proud that I had made a radio which could actually receive. But it was really no big deal. However, because I'd fooled around with radios in my early days, this probably influenced my kid brother. As we grew up, Ernie and I always shared the same bedroom. Over the years, Ernie gathered together and stored enough electronic equipment under the bed to probably make fifteen short wave sets.

He turned out to be one of the leading short-wave "ham" radio operators in the area. He'd talk to people in South America and all over. But he was always bootlegging. He was an unlicensed "ham" all during the time he was in junior high and high school, talking to people all over the world. That was his "habit" and he continued this interest as a grown man.

I remember many years later when he was living in New Jersey, he probably had $20,000 worth of radio equipment in his cellar, possibly more. I have no idea what all that kind of equipment costs. He had such a high aerial for transmitting that the city came out and make him cut off about 25 feet of it to be legal height. He was a great "ham" operator and spent most of his free time in the cellar operating his radio. He'd spend hours and hours contacting other hams, sometimes helping out where there were emergencies.

During the late 1930s, there were after hour places and a lot of musicians out jamming. The great pianist Art Tatum came into town and we became great friends. Art was an aficionado of every sport. He loved them all even though his eyesight was very poor and he could hardly see what was going on. I'd take him to any kind of athletic events that he wanted and he liked just about every one of them.

Art got off work at two in the morning. I was working at Sebastian's and we didn't get off until three. If possible, I'd pick Art up or we'd plan to meet someplace and then we'd go find an after hour club. Then we'd go out and jam almost every night, all night long.

We would start out drinking Pabst Blue Ribbon beer, stack the empty cans on the floor and see if we could pile them up to the ceiling before the evening was over. Usually these sessions were held in private homes. They'd sell whisky in a tea cup and maybe something to eat like a bowl of chili, a bowl of gumbo, maybe some chittlins. We'd always know which one of the places had the best pianos. Art would come in and play with the keys for a while. But after the night was over, they'd have to bring in a piano tuner because Art gave those old pianos such a work out as they'd never had before in their life! It was very exciting musically and I'll always feel grateful for the times I played with Tatum at those jam sessions.

There was a fantastic place over the Club Alabam called the Breakfast Club, which was run by a couple of Italian fellows, the Risotto brothers. They had taken over ownership of the Club Alabam, had an open bar and the place didn't open until two-thirty in the morning (it was illegal in California to serve liquor after two). They also had a gambling table. You could do anything on Central Avenue that you wanted to do if you knew the right politicians and the right policeman in the precinct. The Breakfast Club opened when everyplace else shut down at around two-thirty. They served great fried chicken and hot biscuits with honey. This was a classier place than, for example, the De Liso breakfast club in Chicago. I once brought George Hearst, of the newspaper family there. You'd see big Hollywood stars like the Bennetts, the Talmadges and big time prize fighters like Mickey Walker,who was the middleweight champion of the world. This was typical of the sort of people who frequented the place.

These same people used to come to the Apex, later the Alabam, and to the Breakfast Club, upstairs. That was when Central Avenue was something. People who have only seen it in the last forty years can't imagine how it used to be. It has become a hang-out for misplaced persons from the South and East who came out to California to work in the defense plants, to escape the draft during the war, and stayed. From that time on, Central Avenue became just a place for these people to congregate and was no longer a special place.

I had continued working for Les Hite until he lost the job at Sebastian's Cotton Club when they stopped having shows there. Before Les left town, he got us all together for a special occasion. Count Basie and his band came out to California for the first time in 1939. The entire Les Hite band was at the railway station at 6th and Central to meet the train. We played the *One O'Clock Jump* to welcome the Basie band as they got off the train. We had a fleet of open autos waiting for all the musicians, with pretty girls in each car. The fleet drove from 6th and Central to the Dunbar

Hotel, where Basie was staying. And that's when I first got to know Basie and we got to be pretty good friends. While he was in the Los Angeles area, he liked to go to the race track and we used to run into one another there. So I've known him for a long time.

Basie had come to Los Angeles in 1939 to do a one night stand, or perhaps it was for a week, at the Palomar Ballroom on Vermont Avenue. Preceding Basie at the Palomar was the Charlie Barnet band and one night while they were playing, the place caught on fire and burned down along with their music, instruments and everything. That left Count with no place to play. But it happened that the Paramount Theatre at 6th and Hill was vacant that week, and they put him in there. Up until that time, Basie was an East Coast band and not really known on the West Coast. But the West Coast got to know him when he played the Paramount and he had his first big success there with the big band.

After the Les Hite band fell apart, I skipped around a bit, jobbed around and made what used to be called "race records." These were for the most part made by small groups doing the sort of music that sold well in the southern black areas of the United States, in the beer palaces and such: Rhythm and blues and that type of music. All sorts of people, just anybody who had a blues tune, would try to get their songs recorded. It was simply a question of getting four, five or six people together and making the record. Most of the musicians didn't have a contract and the record companies were little nondescript outfits. Some don't even exist anymore. We would record with whichever company had the best distribution. But it really didn't matter. The important thing was getting a pay check at the end of the date. I never cared about the name of the recording I did or who I was recording with, what or why. I had a big responsibility at home. So it was just "take the money and run". It wasn't all to my taste, because as far as I'm concerned, there are only two types of music: good music and bad music. And a lot of this was not very good.

Also during that time, I worked at practically every movie studio, all the big ones: Warner Brothers, First National, Universal, MGM, you name it, I recorded for all of those. I had no contract. I'd be called by a contractor. They'd call because they

54

knew me and my work but we didn't socialize in the same places. That was one of the disadvantages of having the two unions, a black one and a white one. We didn't have any place to socialize, to get to know each other. We'd be acquainted only on the job if, that is, I was fortunate enough to get that job and work in a mixed group.

Then I started to work regular with Cee Pee Johnson. He was a handsome black man, an entertainer who fronted his band and sang all the vocals. Cee Pee played both a four string guitar and large tom toms which he hit with mallets. And he certainly had a way with the ladies. He was a very, very popular fellow with the other sex and had a string of women going around the corner. All of them loved him and he made it with whoever was there to be had.

Cee Pee Johnson had a fine small band which he took over from Emerson Scott. His group had been working in Long Beach. Alton Redd, Jack McVea and Paul Campbell were the fellows in the Scott band who hit the gray horse in the fog. Emerson Scott, the leader, didn't want to keep a band any more and he took a position in the post office. These were hard times and the post office was a better means of survival, actually a prestigious place to work. Emerson was not the only musician who wanted the steady job and good pay check that the post office offered. Some of the others who left music for the postal service were Marvin Johnson, Charlie Jones, and George Orendorff. A few fellows tried to continue music, too, worked all day and played nights and wound up becoming alcoholics. But Emerson left the music business and, since he was also an alto player, it was actually his chair that I took when I joined the group which was now the Cee Pee Johnson band.

We had three saxophones. There were Jack McVea, Buddy Banks and me on alto, two trumpets, Red Mack and Paul Campbell, Johnny Miller on bass, Alton Redd drums and Herb Williams was the piano player. Johnny Miller was one of the best bass players in town. Later, he left Cee Pee and went with Nat Cole to replace Wesley Prince.

Alton Redd, the drummer, was one of my very dear friends.

He was a nephew of Miss Alma Hightower whom I had worked with occasionally when I was a very young man. In those days, to keep yourself popular, you had to do more than one thing. Besides playing drums, Alton's other forte was singing different types of songs. On some of them, he was quite comical and was very well liked. Besides, Alton had one other important talent. He and Elmer Fain, the business agent with the musician's local, were two fellows who could find more jobs for people to work than anybody else around town.

I remember when Alton and I were both with Atwell Rose, Sunday was our day off but almost every Sunday, Alton would find a job for us. We would play "on stage jazz" with a six-piece band, when those things weren't even known about, in one of the neighborhood theaters. This was about 1929 or 1930 and was a real innovation.

For some reason, one of the trumpet players, Red Mack, left and now there was an opening. My brother Ernie came into the band as a full-time working musician. When Ernie was in his last year of high school, he got married and needed to get a job. The way this happened was that Ernie was one of the sharpest boys in the school and his girl friend was about the prettiest. They started going together and her mother suspected that they were getting pretty intimate and worried that they were having sex. So she went over and had a talk with my mother about it. Well, the girl not only admitted it, she told my mother that she was pregnant. That did it! Ernie did the right thing and married her. Now he needed to bring money home so I got him a job, working with Cee Pee Johnson's band, too. That was the latter part of 1938-39.

Previously, he had worked for a short time one summer with the Les Hite orchestra when we did one of our little tours up and down the coast. Then he went back to school. He had also played now and then with some other young fellows who formed a group called the Woodman Brothers. There we were three Woodman brothers, and they were Britt, who later played trombone with Ellington, Coney and William Woodman. Coney (I think short for Cornelius) was the pianist, and William played sax and trumpet.

The Woodman brothers had their band in the mid-30s when they were all pretty young kids, still in school, and the few little jobs they played most likely were Ernie's first ones.

Their usual bass player was Charlie Mingus who I first met when he and Ernie were working with the Woodman Brothers Orchestra. Mingus was about a year younger than Ernie, so I didn't ever know him well. Those fellows all grew up in Watts, a mostly black suburb south of Los Angeles. Charlie was always a very hyper person even as a young man, what we'd call now "way-out." They say genius and insanity are brothers and you really had the two brothers there with Mingus. He was close to being as radically out of it as anybody, but he certainly had a spark of genius attached to him, too. As a child and as a young man, he was always a very good bass player. He was fast, and he could take solos almost like a horn. He came up around the same time as Joe Comfort, who also grew up in the Watts area, and the two of them would sort of interlock and exchange jobs in places with the Woodman Brothers Orchestra. The kids never had any regular jobs, though, just played an occasional date.

Mingus later took a few lessons from Red Callender, but before that he could play very well and had a lot on the ball even when he was a young kid. However, he was so radical that a lot of people were afraid to hire him after he got a little older. Lionel put him in his big band for a time but Mingus cut his ties with Hampton when they got to the New York area and stayed there, jobbing around.

Many, many years later when I was playing at the Apollo Theater in New York with the Basie band, one day Lawrence Brown came down to see me and said, "we are fixing to lose our bass player and we're going to have to find a new one. Do you know anybody you can recommend?" So I told him "I know a fellow I can recommend to you for his playing qualities but as far as his actions around people go, I can't say I approve of that. But if you want, tell Duke it would be good if he could go listen to this young fellow, Charlie Mingus." So that's how Mingus got his job with Ellington. But he didn't stay with Duke very long, either.

Going back to when Ernie was about fifteen, I taught him

how to drive, and I had gotten him a driver's license. At the time, I had a brand new 1936 De Soto automobile which I had had modified by the Miller Autoworks, the people who rebuilt cars for the Indianapolis races. It could go astonishingly fast, about 125 miles an hour. I left the car at home when I had to go on a tour with Les Hite for maybe six weeks and told my mother that if it was really necessary, she should allow my brother to drive her where she needed to go. My brother persuaded my mother that it was *very* necessary for him to use the car to get to work with one of the Woodman Brothers.

He took my brand new De Soto and loaded it down with members of the orchestra, about seven of them with their instruments, in my five passenger automobile. My brother managed to turn the car over and roll it with the seven guys inside. They were packed in so tight that none of them was hurt with the exception of one fellow who got a little scratch on his arm!

In those days, we people who lived over on the east side of Los Angeles could not get decent insurance so I had to pay for everything the car needed out of my pocket. It was in the shop getting repaired for a long time and it took about another month before they could get it together right. I wasn't mad at Ernie, and I didn't strike him or anything because he was my brother and I was just glad that he hadn't been hurt. We were very, very close brothers; in fact they used to call us the Corsican Brothers meaning if one was hurt, the other one would feel it even from a distance.

The other trumpet player when Ernie started with Cee Pee was Paul Campbell. He was out of St. Louis and an excellent player, could do his job and play good jazz as well as legitimate trumpet and good leads. Some time later, he had to leave Cee Pee to take care of his mother, who was ill at the time. After he left, he went back and worked with the Jeter and Pillars band, which was the group he had been with previously. This was a territory band in the St. Louis area with two leaders, James Jeter and Charles Pillars. Other musicians who were in this group at one time or another were Clark Terry and Ahmad Jamal.

With all of these fine musicians, Cee Pee Johnson had such a good little band that other musicians came out to hear us. First we worked on Main Street at the Paradise, replacing Lionel's group when he went with Benny Goodman. Nat "King" Cole was one of the people who liked to come in and play with us. As soon as Nat got off work from his own job, he'd be sitting in. Partly this is because it was Nat's own arrangements we were playing! At the time, King Cole was writing arrangements for several girl singers. Among these was Juanelda Carter who later changed her name to Judy Caroll and became quite well-known. We had taken Nat's whole book of arrangements for Juanelda and revised them for the band.

Incidentally, in those years Nat was an underpaid musician with his original trio. He had Oscar Moore on guitar and Wesley Prince from Pasadena on bass. But Nat was ambitious and had a few talks with Carlos Gastel, who was a personal manager. Carlos told him, "When you get to the place that I can demand $300 a week for you, then I will manage you." Well, Nat got bigger and that's how Gastel came to be his manager.

After the Paradise engagement, Cee Pee's band was hired to open a new club on Highland Avenue in Hollywood which was owned by the same man who had the chain of Chili Bowls restaurants. In the 1920's and 30's, Los Angeles used to be famous for restaurants that looked like an object. There was the Brown Derby restaurant in the shape of a hat and the Tail of the Pup, which served hot dogs and was in a building that looked like a big dog. And then there were several Chili Bowl restaurants dotted around town. These were round, white, free-standing buildings that resembled the sort of bowl you'd serve chili in. I think this club in Hollywood was his first night club and it later was called the Rhum Boogie. It was typical of clubs in those days, with a band for dancing, a show with a chorus line and so on.

A short while after Ernie came to work for Cee Pee, it turned out there was a little bit of a discrepancy about why my brother, who was still a minor, should be married to this young girl. I found out she really wasn't pregnant so I went over to the house one day and brought him back home. We got an annulment of the marriage and he moved back into the family house.

As it happens, we only remained together as a family for a very short time. My sister La Verne got married in 1939 and went to live in New York. She never did do anything with music, although I imagine she was talented and she had a lovely singing voice. Then, my mother remarried in 1940. After the family dwindled, I rented an apartment and took my eighteen year old brother with me. We stayed together for the next several years and often worked together. Ernie and I were with Cee Pee's band right into 1940 when we both left to join Hampton.

The man my sister married worked as a waiter on the railroad and through him, I had the privilege of meeting a very famous classical pianist, Ignatz Paderewski. During those years, from 1910 or so until after World War II, the elegant way to travel was by private railroad car. Notables had their own car to go from coast to coast. My brother-in-law, Schuyler Wise, traveled on these private cars, along with a couple of cooks and stewards. He did the serving and filled out the menus for whoever happened to be on the private car. He was a very classy type New Yorker and I still remember how he ate fish, boning it elegantly with a knife and fork. Schuyler was working on Paderewski's private railroad car at that particular time.

I liked those big threequarter-inch ham steaks they always used to have on those private cars. So I'd go down to see Schuyler on his car, have breakfast with him and we'd talk. Over breakfast one morning, he introduced me to Paderewski, who was an outstanding classical pianist and at one time was a candidate for president of Poland. He understood English very well although he never got to the place where he spoke it easily. But we managed to talk together well enough that I was able to tell him about a wonderful artist I'd like for him to hear.

Paderewski, fortunately, always carried two pianos in his private car. He said, "Very good. Bring him down. I'd love to hear him."

The person I was referring to was, of course, Art Tatum. I went and told Art I'd like for him to go down and play for Paderewski. Art said, "Sure, I'd be glad to do that."

We arranged to go the next morning. When Art got there, the two men were introduced to each other and Art was invited to play. He sat down at the piano and played for about an hour and a half without stopping. He ran through his repertoire from the classics on through boogie-woogie, swing, and all the popular songs in his own particular marvelous way. Paderewski was astounded. Tears were actually coming out of his eyes. When Art finished playing, Paderewski said,"Mr. Tatum, if you had applied all of your time toward being a classical pianist, there would have been nobody in the entire world who could have surpassed you in your way of playing." As we were leaving, he shook Tatum's hand almost off his arm, in his delight at meeting and hearing him.

It was customary those years on Labor Day to have a big parade in downtown Los Angeles all the way down Broadway, with bands, of course. I was put in charge of the big band for local 767 that year. That was the black union. The white union was number 47. Instead of us walking all that way, I rented a great big flat bed truck that would hold 35 or 40 people. I fitted about a 35-piece band, the official 767 Musician's Union band, on that truck.

With that many men, I doubled up the instruments. Instead of having four or five saxes, I had ten of them; trumpets, instead of four I had eight; six or eight trombones, my piano player was Nat "King" Cole. We had two basses. One was Wesley Prince, Nat's bass man, and Red Callender was the other. We also got in touch with Count Basie and Jimmie Lunceford, who were in town, and got them to play for that same parade. So the black union hired two more trucks. My band led the way, Count Basie was second and Lunceford was the third band.

When we finished the route downtown, we rode that big flat-bed truck back toward the Musician's Union, which always put on a big barbecue afterwards. As we drove, we passed Lionel Hampton's house, that is, his mother-in-law's place on 10th Street. We stopped outside to play a little serenade for him. Lionel never forgot this and later, when he left Benny Goodman, he tried to hire the whole damn band that he heard that day! He contacted me, and that's how I became his sort of music director.

61

6
With Lionel

Not too much later in 1940, I helped Lionel (always pronounced Lion-EL) form his band. He really intended to have seventeen pieces playing whole-note harmonies while he played his vibraphones. I don't think anybody would have stood for that but he might have had some success. I rehearsed that band for him down at my old stomping ground, the Club Alabam, while he stood over to the side and watched.

When we first started out, Lionel hardly had any book at all. He came into the band business with just some take-offs on things he had done with Benny Goodman. He was sextet-minded. Sometimes, the sextet within the new group would play for 15 or 20 minutes before the band ever came in. That was his idea of a big band, which was entirely wrong as far as I was concerned. The first week that we started rehearsing, his repertoire was sterile, just nothing. I introduced him to an arranger, a fellow we called the Fox, whose real name was George Williams. The Fox worked day and night for five days making arrangements and just like that, we had a book. This is how Lionel Hampton's band was made ready to go on the road. Our first engagement was on October 6, 1940.

Ray Perry and I both played sax and doubled on violin. Ray was an established violinist from Boston; very, very good. The two of us played the ballads on electrified fiddles, along with the three clarinets. On guitar was Irving Ashby out of Boston, a good electric guitar player. We also had an electric bass, the first one made, which looked like a stick. Vernon Alley from San Francisco played it. And of course Lionel's vibes were electric, too. Somebody said this was the first all-electric band.

Vernon Alley, the bassist, and I became close friends and he grew to be like a second brother to me. We first met when I was up in San Francisco with the Mosby band. Vernon was a young teen-ager then, still going to high school. He was a football player, well-built, light-skinned with freckles. Vernon found some kind of way to meet me at that time and we became friends. Now we played together in the Hampton band and again, later, in the Navy. Vernon is a true San Franciscan and could never stay away from there for long. Well, Los Angeles is not that far from San Francisco and we always stay in touch by telephone if our paths do not cross otherwise. We've remained friends throughout the years and I respect him for being a fine musician and a true gentleman.

In the Hampton band reed section, we had five saxophones. I played lead and Ray Perry was the second alto. To explain, the lead person is the one who carries the melody, one of its many inversions or part of the chord.

Our first tenor man was Bob Barfield from San Francisco, an excellent player and a very nice man but he was only with the band a short time. He went all the way to Vancouver, Canada with us. But Bob had a couple of problems. He drank a whole lot of whiskey and his marriage life wasn't complete. He had female trouble. When we came back through San Francisco, his wife gave him a bad time and that's when he left us.

We decided to try Dexter Gordon as his replacement on tenor. Dexter's father was my doctor and a personal friend of the family. Besides that, my brother and Dexter had gone to Jefferson High school at the same time and they knew each other, although Dexter was younger and would have been just starting about the time Ernie was graduating. So I recommended Dexter to Lionel and he joined us.

Jack McVea, who played baritone in the band, came up with Lorenzo and Otis Flennoy and me. We all lived within a hundred yards of each other as children. Jack was always a good sax and clarinet player and had always kept busy working. He was with Charlie Echols, with Emerson Scott and then with Cee Pee. He joined the Lionel Hampton band when it was first formed in 1940. At that time, I would have not considered anyone better on the baritone saxophone than Jack, excepting for Harry Carney. Jack will always be remembered for his song *Open the Door Richard*.

The other tenor saxophone player was Illinois Jacquet. This little fellow from Louisiana proved to be an influential member of the band. He had a vivacious personality and his tenor saxophone voice was an important part of the hot playing.

In the brass section, our lead trumpet was Jack Trainer, a Los Angeles musician. He was a husky fellow with a scar on one cheek. A fellow from Texas, called Goo Goo was another trumpet and my kid brother Ernie was a standout because he could play lead as well as solos.

Within a few months of the time the band was formed, we did our first Southern tour and ran across another good trumpet player, a young fellow who was going to Alabama State College. His name was Joe Newman. Lionel hired him after Joe came down and auditioned for us in Atlanta, Georgia. For the first time we had four trumpets in the band.

The trombone section was outstanding. There was Sonny Craven who had played trombone with the Les Hite band and who could do the wah-wah plunger things like Joe "Tricky Sam" Nanton with Ellington. We called him Mush Mouth. Fred Becket, originally out of Tupelo, Mississippi, could play trombone just as sweet and pretty as anyone who ever lived. He was wonderful. The third trombone was a Houston musician named Henry Sloan, who was sort of a comedian. He'd come out and sing a little tune, do a little dance. This went over big with Lionel, who was always an exhibitionist, himself.

To sum it up, the Hampton band was a fiery young group of fellows with a lot of vinegar. To show you how young they were, my brother was not quite twenty at the time the band formed and Irving Ashby and Illinois Jacquet were about the same age. Ray Perry and Vernon Alley were maybe twenty-one or twenty-two. When Dexter Gordon joined us, he was the baby. I don't think he was even eighteen years old yet.

Organizing a new band, you don't always wind up with the same men you started with. Change-overs happen in an orchestra in the beginning because sometimes people join and then find that they don't really like something about it. It's not that they get fired, it's just that they don't dovetail together and then there's a parting of the ways.

Lee Young, Lester's brother, was the drummer with our

original group. He took the first trip with the band but he wasn't happy. His replacement was Shadow Wilson, a New York and Philadelphia area drummer, but Shadow only lasted with us about a year. He had a problem with abuse of alcohol and other things.

After he left, following Shadow Wilson on drums was the young man who married Dinah Washington and was the father of her child. His name was George Jenkins.

We began with Sir Charles Thompson on piano, but at that time there was no "Sir" in front of his name. He was simply Charles Thompson. He added the "Sir" later on down the line. While he was with Hamp, he was not only known as a good pianist but also as an arranger. His work was always in very good taste so we enjoyed playing the few arrangements he did. As I recall, he didn't make that many, perhaps three or four at the most. Before the first year was out, he made different plans. Sir Charles' preference was to play solo piano. However, during the war, he played with the Illinois Jacquet small band. During that time, he composed the well-known tune *Robbins' Nest*.

About four months after Sir Charles left the band, a wonderful pianist named Milt Buckner joined us. He was the brother of the Teddy Buckner who was the noted alto saxophone player in the Jimmie Lunceford band. Milt was one of the top arrangers in the country and, from the time he joined us, did many of our arrangements.

The predominant thing in Lionel Hampton's life was playing his vibraphone, which he did better than anybody else in the world. And he didn't think much about anything else. Luckily, his wife Gladys was on top of things. She kept him straight-laced to the extent that people thought she was too strict with him. This was impossible! All the strictness she could think of was truly necessary to keep him on the straight and narrow. All during the time he was with Goodman and then with his own band, she was right there keeping him on his toes and looking after him.

Gladys stayed behind the scenes, though. Previously, her business had been making clothes for people like Joan Crawford, the Talmadge Sisters and other big movie actresses of that time and she was a first-rate seamstress. Luckily, Gladys also had a very good business head on her because Lionel didn't have any business head at all.

Lionel's wife really looked out after him and made him a financial success. In fact, she actually made him a rich man! During the time before the United States entered World War Two, all during early 1941 and even after we entered the war, Gladys bought at least one $1000 government bond every week we were working. I know, because I often used to go with her to the bank to deposit the money. She was salting it away.

I remember an unusual occurrence when we were playing the Regal Theater in Chicago. We were off-stage ready to start the performance, just waiting for the curtain to be raised when all of a sudden we heard an argument in the wings. Gladys and Lionel were having heated words! This was a rarity between the two because usually Gladys did all of the talking and Lionel did all of the listening. But this particular time, Lionel was refusing to go on stage and perform unless Gladys allowed him $5 a day for spending money. And he stayed off-stage until Gladys agreed that she would give him the $5 a day. That's how tight she was with him.

Of course, she always kept enough out to buy herself some furs. Gladys had all of the best furs there were, a different fur for every day in the month. Nobody in the United States had more or better furs than Gladys Hampton. She also bought an eight unit building on Adams Boulevard in Los Angeles. She took two of the units and combined them into a place for their own personal dwelling. The other six she rented out and let the property appreciate in value over the years. It turned out to be very valuable. Yes, Gladys was a beautiful help to Lionel, making sure he was well taken care of and his money was always put in the right places. Fortunately for him, she fixed it so he never had to ask favors of anyone, because he had his own money.

The Hampton band began its first extended tour in December 1941. First we played in Texas, appearing at Dallas, Galveston, Houston, El Paso, San Antonio, Fort Worth and all the big cities. Seeing the south for the first time was quite an experience for me. I had lived with pseudo jim crow in California for many years and I knew what that was all about but it was quite a shock to find out exactly how far apart people of color and white people lived in the south. It was two different worlds!

In Fort Worth, the hotel where we stayed was in the middle of the ghetto, and it was called the Gem. Some gem! It was positively the worst hotel I have ever stayed at in my entire life. It was hot, but there was no air conditioning of any kind excepting for any air that might come in through the screens on all the doors. Torn screens. If a wind blew, you got cooled off a little. It was dusty and dirty and everything about it was just terrible.

Then, we went to New Orleans. This is supposed to be the hot bed, the start, the beginning, of where jazz was created. As far as I am concerned, it's hard for any man in his right mind to put his finger on when jazz began. To start with, nobody knows exactly what jazz is, probably nobody knows what the word jazz stands for, nor who the person was who named that type of music "jazz."

In the early days, around the turn of the century, my father was a musician on the riverboats going up to St.Louis. People playing that type of music in those days called it "ragtime." Maybe ragtime started in New Orleans. I'm not a historian, I don't know that much about it, all I can do is relate things as they were told to me by older people. Practically all the New Orleans musicians who were any good had moved out to someplace else where they could make it, where it was better for their careers.

Some of these men had moved to California to have a better life. When I was quite young, I saw and heard Kid Ory, Papa Mutt Carey, and some of the other New Orleans musicians. These were mostly older men, much older than my father, born back in the 1860s and all long gone. My dad made sure that I heard this music and all kinds of music so I'd have a rounded musical background. From time to time, he took me to hear the New Orleans men play at penny dance places around Los Angeles.

In California, our music was a hodge podge of this and that. We didn't have that many Dixieland bands. There were differences in style between eastern and western musicians in the early days because we didn't get to hear one another. Before planes, going 3000 miles from New York to Los Angeles would ordinarily mean nearly a week of travel so we didn't have a chance to influence each other. The only traveling bands that ever came to California in the early days, name bands that is, were Duke Ellington, McKinney's Cotton Pickers and Cab Calloway, who all came out in the 30s. For instance, as wonderful a saxophone player as Benny Carter was, I never heard a record to know it was him playing until 1939 or 1940, although he played wonderful sax for many years before that.

Harry Carney and I were good friends when the Ellington band first came out here. He said to me in 1930, "You sure remind me of Benny Carter," and I didn't know who Benny Carter was! A couple of years later, McKinney's Cotton Pickers were out in Los Angeles before I joined Les. Don Redman, leader of the saxophone section and arranger, heard me playing at a rehearsal, something I was doing with Les, and he said, "You certainly remind me of Benny Carter." And again, I didn't know who he was talking about.

Then I heard Benny on his tune *When Lights are Low*, which he made with Lionel. The same year I heard a record made under Benny's own name called *Sleep*. Before that, I probably heard him but not to know who he actually was. I never even met Benny until he hired me to play in a band he was getting together for a show sometime after World War II. Until I came across Louis Armstrong as the perfect exponent of the trumpet, which he was, I never knew about referring to the New Orleans type of music as "jazz." Saying that New Orleans was the the beginning of jazz, it seems to me that it's all according to the year that you want to recognize a particular kind of music as being jazz.

Just as there were a few excellent musicians who came out of the New Orleans area, there were just as many or more bad ones who came from there. As I was coming up, I had the misfortune of playing in pick-up groups, not organized bands, where sometimes one of these New Orleans musicians would be listed as appearing in the same band I was to work with. In my childhood, as I've said, the music they played was called ragtime and many times, these people didn't know one thing about reading music. They only played by ear. There is nothing wrong at all with playing by ear but you can only play certain things that way. The world moved on, orchestras started getting bigger, and a professional musician should really have known how to put a few chords together besides playing single-note melodies.

When I first got to New Orleans in January of 1941, there were no big bands down there at all and very few small ones, either. Up until today, there have been very few organized bands to come out of there. The only people making a living playing music are around the French Quarter in clubs with Dixieland bands. Seemingly anyone who knew how to play well had left, gone east or west or north or somewhere to make more money. I didn't hear hardly any good players when I as there.

We went on to Florida, where it was another completely segregated world. If a black person wanted to go out on Miami Beach, he had to have a license with his picture on it! That was a new experience for me. We went on up through the Carolinas and finally got into New York. This city is always an eye opener for an out of towner, especially looking up at those high buildings down town. We didn't work downtown, though. We did a few dates around the area and jumped straight into Chicago, where we played the Grand Terrace.

New York was never one of my favorite cities. I think it is one of the world's most over-rated places, along with Paris. I've always thought that people made cities, but New York and Paris make the people. However, Chicago was a different story. The blacks in Chicago had a different way to live. Through their need for survival, they had started their own businesses, cab companies, and so on. Some others made nice salaries and lived very well on the South Side of Chicago, too. Alderman and people of importance stood up for the black people there. In my eyes, Chicago was always one of the better places for a black man to stop if he wanted to improve his position in life. With a little bit of help and plenty of hard work, a person could have a pretty good lifestyle there.

During my years with Hampton, I acted as musical director

and that meant that I was out front as announcer for shows whenever Lionel himself was not out there with his vibraphone. On one of our trips to Chicago, we were playing in the Panther Room of the Hotel Sherman. Billie Holiday was the featured artist on the bill. When we went into rehearsals with Billie and her music, Lionel took me aside and said, "Now you bring Billie Holiday on as featured artist, but don't give her no encores!"

I caught on right away and answered "Well, you've got it, old dude."

So that night, opening night, Billie came on and she did her act, sang two or three tunes and went off. The audience loved her and the applause was deafening. I brought her back to take a bow. She came back very graciously and took a bow and went off again. The people were still applauding so I brought her back to take another bow. I looked over to the piano player and told him to play the introduction to whatever tune it was she had selected for an encore. Billie went back on, and broke it up again. She was just a terrific success. When she went off stage, wonderful applause followed her. She came back and took another bow. The applause continued so I started the band off for her second encore. She did her song and the audience again applauded loudly. When she came off, she was so happy that she threw her arms around me and thanked me warmly.

Lionel was scheduled to follow her. He came on and he was just livid. He was absolutely furious that I had allowed this woman to take two encores in front of him. But by my doing that, Billie and I formed a friendship that probably lasted until she died. We were always the best of friends.

Gladys had gotten Lionel interested in politics, in becoming a figurehead with the Republican party through acquaintances of hers in Los Angeles political circles. She knew one of the Supervisors, which put her into a good position with the Republican party. Gladys was open minded when it came to getting knowledge about the world

Through the connections that Gladys Hampton had with her political acquaintances, she was invited to an important luncheon at the Rosenthal Foundation in Chicago in 1941. She asked me to accompany her because, at that time, Lionel was not particularly interested in political affairs. Some of Chicago's better known people attended and the honored person at that meeting was Mrs. Eleanor Roosevelt. I had a chance to meet her and it was a pleasure having the opportunity of seeing people in the upper echelons of politics.

Not too long ago, I read an article about an inquiry at HUD (Housing and Urban Development,) which is supposed to lend money to low income people to help them obtain housing. It seems that someone in the top management there had granted Lionel a loan for 21 million dollars as an advance on 69 apartments he was putting up! That was in the *Los Angeles Times* on August 29, 1989. It looks like Gladys taught him well, because he has been on his own for a long time now. Gladys, who was quite a lot older than Lionel, died many years ago. She was born, I believe, in 1899, and Lionel in 1907 or 1908.

I knew Gladys for a long time before Lionel did, because my mother helped to raise her. They were both from Denison, Texas. Lionel named a tune *Rock Hill Special* for the area of Denison where Gladys grew up. She and I always got along very well and I respected her as the first-class lady that she was.

Hamp learned early on that it was good politics to name tunes after disc jockeys. The first was *Jack the Bell Boy*, named for a well-known late night disc jockey in Los Angeles, which he recorded with just the King Cole trio and a drummer before the big band was formed. Nat Cole played piano chords behind Lionel's one-finger jamming on the piano. Later, the band recorded a tune of mine which was named after a San Francisco radio show called *Open House* . About the same time we recorded *Fiddle Dee Dee*. This particular tune was also mine and we did it more than once, with Ray Perry on the fiddle and me on the clarinet. I never got a penny from any of my things, never got residuals, royalties or anything. Everything went to Lionel.

There were a lot of originals done by fellows in the band. All of the things the sextet played were little tunes we just made up at the studio. I remember Irving Ashby's name was on one and I'm under the impression that this was rather unusual. Although these things were really put together by the fellows, Lionel's name most likely appears on the records as composer.

We didn't have arrangements on all our tunes. *Flying Home* is one of the numbers on which we didn't have a written arrangement. I have a vivid recollection of the day we made the record of this tune. We had usually started out with the six piece jam band; Lionel on his vibes, plus a violin, a guitar, a clarinet, bass, and drums. When we'd get on stage, we might play five, ten, even fifteen minutes before the band ever came back in.

But when we recorded the number, it had to be condensed down to fit the three minute time limit on ten inch records. It was Jacquet's exciting solo on the tune which made this a hit record for us. I think it actually was our first big hit record. The other tune we recorded at that session was *In the Bag*.

By coincidence, there was an important happening that day. We were recording in a studio which was high up on the 34th floor of a building in downtown Manhattan. Through the windows, we could see New York's harbor where all the big ships were docked. While we watched, the *Normandie*, a famed passenger ship of that time, burst into flames and we saw it burning. In between doing takes on *Flying Home* and looking out the window, this important passenger ship turned over on the side in the harbor. The firemen had poured so much water on it that the ship lost balance! That's a sight none of us will ever forget.

I stayed with Hampton from 1940 until the First of September 1942. In the late summer of 1942, we were back in Los Angeles playing the Orpheum Theater. During the intermission between the shows, I was resting backstage in a quiet corner and suddenly I heard voices on the other side of the screen. It was Gladys Hampton speaking to Joe Glaser, the booking agent. I didn't think anything of it and didn't feel as if I should say "I'm back here."

During the course of their conversation, Joe Glaser told Gladys. "The way to make this band a success is to buy the men as cheap as you can and sell them as expensive as you can."

I didn't say a word, just stayed there. When they got through talking, I went out from behind the curtain and said "Joe, I heard your conversation. Very enlightening." I added: "You won't have to be bothered with me very long because I'm 1-A in the draft and will be leaving soon, anyway. I might as well quit now."

He said, "You can't afford to quit us! I'll have you put on the no hire list. Won't nobody hire you."

I answered, "I'll have to take a chance on that," and added a little bit of profanity to let him know what I thought about him. They never paid any big money in that band anyway. The most I ever made in the Lionel Hampton band was $14 a night.

My brother Ernie was blowing most of the hot trumpet solos in the band. He said, "If you're leaving, I'm leaving, too." So we both departed at the conclusion of the engagement at the Orpheum Theater and signed up with the Navy. I never went back with Lionel again.

7
The Navy And After

During the time I was with the Hampton band, we got into World War II. I remember hearing on the radio about the Pearl Harbor attack. We were in Jersey at the time and had to catch the subway for our engagement at the Strand Theater in Brooklyn. From that time on, while we were traveling on the road I kept receiving reminders that I should come down to my draft board and have a few words with them as soon as I was in Los Angeles. I was 1-A, healthy, and just about the right age for the Army to grab me. Actually, I was offered a warrant officer's job in the Army at Camp Mead, Maryland. But I didn't take it. I saw these men coming back from a training session, mud up to their knees, and I knew I wouldn't like that so I decided to enlist in the Navy instead.

It was the first time that black musicians ever were afforded the opportunity to be in the Navy as musicians. Up to that time, all blacks in the Navy served the officers as steward's mates or some other type of menial work, being non-participants in fighting and working practically as servants.

By enlisting, I figured I'd have a chance to choose a bit. It was October 1942 when my brother Ernie and I went down to enlist. While he was passing the physical with flying colors, the doctors examined me and shook their heads. I think it was my high blood pressure they didn't like. Poor Ernie had this worried expression on his face as he saw me being taken out of the line. They told me to come back the next day. When I went back, without further tests, they accepted me. Obviously somebody knew my work as a musician and they wanted me. Just like that, I was in the Navy.

Such famous musicians as Artie Shaw and Glenn Miller received recognition going into the service, but it didn't happen to me or any other black musician. In World War II, everyone that enlisted in the Navy as a musician was sent to Camp Roberts Smalls for assignment. This was at the Great Lakes Naval Station, just South of Chicago, and was something new, the

Navy's first grouping of black musicians.

The people who came into the group at the same time as I did were mostly from the San Francisco area. This is where the enlistment office was and the particularly talented musicians were sent to Camp Roberts Smalls. These included Vernon Alley, my friend from the Hampton band, (who was like a brother to Ernie and me), Jerome Richardson, a good reed man who was only about nineteen years old and Wilbert Baranco, a first rate pianist and arranger who also did vocals. There were also a few local musicians from the San Francisco and Oakland area such as young Earl Watkins, who was an excellent drummer, Curtis Lowe, and Quedellus Martin, who is now living in Hawaii.

Besides them, we had quite a few players conscripted from the Los Angeles area, including my brother Ernie and me, Jackie Kelson, now known as Kelso; Buddy Collette, and Andy Anderson, who was a very good tenor saxophone player and worked around the Los Angeles area for years. They put us all together and shipped us to Great Lakes for indoctrination.

Our indoctrination only amounted to being quarantined while we had lots of inoculations to make us immune in case we had to go into areas where there was yellow fever or malaria, plus the usual precautions against tetanus. We were there four weeks before we even got a single day off to go into town or anything. The Chief Petty Officer who signed us all up was very smart because he kept trying to get us out of Great Lakes as a group as soon as possible. Our group was assigned to be stationed at Camp St. Mary's Preflight School on the grounds of St. Mary's College in Orinda, California. He didn't want us hanging around the Great Lakes Naval Station, which would let the Chief Petty Officer for the regular band have an opportunity to pick through us and take out the better people for ship's service. The regular band that they had at Great Lakes included some very, very good musicians. Some of these were Clark Terry, the trumpet player, who came in with the whole group of St. Louis musicians. Later Willie Smith and Gerald Wilson from the Jimmie Lunceford band were there and several other excellent people .

Before the fifth week was up, our Chief Petty Officer

managed to get us out of there and into California at St. Mary's Preflight. We spent the entire duration of the war on the campus there and never had any contact with the enemy. We had a fine group of musicians overall, and we played well. But when it came to marching, it was a farce! We were ridiculous. We looked like forty-five comedians out there trying to march in formation. To give you an idea, one guy in our group, a trombone player, would actually be trying to march with a fifth of liquor in his sock!

I went in with the rank of First Class Seaman and during my three years in the Navy, I was the "assistant" leader of the 45-piece military band. That was because a First Class Seaman did not have rank to be a leader. Only a chief could be leader and, at that time, there were no black musicians who were chiefs in the Navy. The "leader" was a white fellow, a Chief Petty Officer.

Primarily, our 45-piece band was expected to play military music. We recorded every week for the Office of War Information. These discs were played on all the battleships and overseas radio stations and my name appears on them as leader. The discs were never supposed to get into civilian hands but, as will happen, several of them were subsequently issued and sold. I've had calls from people as far away as Australia and New Zealand asking me about them. Some people made thousands of dollars releasing the discs commercially, but of course we Navy musicians never saw a penny of that.

Out of that 45-piece group, we had some smaller groups as well as two dance bands which were known as number one and number two. I was leader of the number one band and got a hold of many, many music scores from the Basie repertoire. We also had some charts written by the arranger, Gerald Wilson and other musicians in the Great Lakes Navy band for blacks. Our number one band played music for dancing. One of the cute things we did was a parody on *Poor Butterfly*, which we selected because we were at war with Japan. In our version, it was *Big Fat Butterfly*, with new lyrics to match. We had the best musicians there were around in those days. This was because most younger musicians in the United States were draft age, including a lot of the finest musicians in the country, and they naturally wound up in the service in some band. Our group at St. Mary's Preflight was an excellent, professional sounding band. It was very, very successful, worth listening to, and well received. No regular commercial band of the time could stand the competition of coming near us when we were appearing.

Throughout the war, we remained at St. Mary's or in the immediate vicinity. One of the main reasons was that our Captain refused to let us get too far away from our home base, not even permitting us to play in Hollywood at the Stage Door Canteen after we had been requested by Bette Davis and some of the other stars. The Captain was afraid that if one of the Admirals heard us, he might steal our band, reassign us to Wake Island or someplace in the South Pacific as his own personal band, for his entertainment. We played performances for soldiers, sailors and marines in various towns where they'd have a place to go and dance.

The cadets came into the base and probably stayed two or three months before they even got a day of liberty. They were required to stay on base and not even allowed to leave for entertainment. So it was up to us to provide it. Those of us who were part of "ship's service", on the other hand, were allowed to leave and could even live off-base if we chose to, as I did. I received an allocation for my room and board and books of food stamps from the Navy .

Our day started every morning at eight when the entire 45-piece band played for flag raising. Then we went back to our barracks for a coffee break. After that, we would rehearse for around three hours every day religiously. Then it was time to play for the cadets to march in formation at noon-time for thirty minutes as they went to lunch. After that, we would go in and eat the same food as the young officers were given. Things like filet mignon were on the regular menu at the base, so many people called it the country club of the Navy. We got the best food there was, in any amount. By then I had a wife and a dog, Mike. Sometimes there was enough to take home extra for them!

After the noon meal, we'd go back and rehearse again and by four in the afternoon, we were through for the day. Then, I'd get into my car and drive back over the Bay Bridge to where I was staying in San Francisco, 26 miles away. I had my own car there and a gas allowance. I was permitted to buy gas on the base at the naval price, which was only a few cents a gallon.

Then, every Sunday, we played for dancing and happy hour for the cadets. One time, we played for a group at Treasure Island. The Admiral there took a liking to me and in the course of a little conversation, I told him I liked to fish. He said, "That's just fine, you can use my boat if you want."

I got a group of fellows together out of the band and the captain gave me his launch for the day. He had ordered special food for us and had about ten enlisted men to wait on us. They supplied us with fishing gear and bait while we went up and down the San Francisco bay trolling in the launch. It was a wonderful day which I'll never forget.

The day was also memorable because we did not get many leaves. In fact, throughout the year we had only two or three weeks off which we could take either split or all at once.

Both Ernie and I got married while we were in the Navy. Ernie married first in 1943, to Florian Douceau, a girl he had known in Los Angeles, whose family came from New Orleans. I got married to a long-time lady friend while I was taking a long leave. She was the singer I saw in 1934 in Seattle, during the first tour up the coast with Les Hite when her name was Evelyn Williamson. When the Hite band made a later tour, Evelyn was singing at the Rhum Boogie Club, another one of her brother-in-law's places. That was in 1938 and at that time, Les hired her to be band vocalist. She came into town with Les and traveled with the band for about a year. She and Bumps Myers got married but the marriage didn't last very long. Then, when the Les Hite band was disintegrating and things went bad, Evelyn stayed in Los Angeles and worked locally.

There was a nice, small bistro, called the Memo, one block away from the Alabam on Central Avenue. It got going about 1938-39 and Evelyn was one of the first singers ever to work there, with Harvey Brooks as her accompanist. Evelyn was a good entertainer, very well liked. She and Harvey made top

78

money there.

About that time, I was going with a lady who had a business in Honolulu. That relationship dissolved when Evelyn was free and we started going together. When Lionel Hampton formed the big band in 1940, Evelyn became his first band vocalist. Over those years, we were out on the road together a lot and had gotten to know each other real well.

Back in those days, there wouldn't be any hotels for blacks. The jim crow was really crowing. When we'd stop in little towns, there'd be no hotels for us. Lionel didn't have anybody looking out for a place for the fellows to stay; It was sort of first come, first serve. We'd have to find a room someplace. You'd start going around to homes in the neighborhood and asking folks to get up out of their bed and let us sleep there. A girl can't do that so I'd get a room with my brother Ernie, and we'd find Evelyn a room, too. After a while, we got to be pretty tight.

In Los Angeles, Evelyn rented a room from Harold Brown and his wife Nellie, who had a house on the East side of town on Vernon Avenue. As soon as the Hampton band returned to Los Angeles, I moved into Harold and Nellie's, too, to be with Evelyn.

Nellie Brown and Evelyn were good friends. Furthermore, Harold had occasionally accompanied Evelyn on the piano and they had worked together at some pretty nice spots. Harold Brown was Lawrence Brown's piano-playing brother and he was a first-rate pianist. I've always thought that he was one of the unsung musicians, an all-around man, well versed as a solo player as well as a first-rate accompanist.

I had known Harold for years, going back to the time when we were both with the Atwell Rose band. Later, during all the years while I was with Les Hite, Harold played at Sebastian's Cotton Club, too, so we were long-time good friends. To give you an idea about his talent, in the 1970s he played at the exclusive Beverly Wilshire Hotel and the engagement lasted for about 15 years!

Back in the forties, Nellie Brown would throw a big party every time the Ellington band came to town. At the time that I was staying at the house, I remember that the party for the Ellington band included about a dozen of the best piano players you could find. All the local fellows were there like Eddie Beal as well as some really great pianists that were in town like the boogie-woogie pianist Meade "Lux" Lewis, Nat "King" Cole, who was undoubtedly one of the greatest piano players of that time, and everyone else who even thought he was a good piano player was at that particular party. After they had all played and done their best it was just about daybreak. Everybody had eaten up everything there was to eat and drunk up everything there was to drink when it finally got to be time for the real champion, Art Tatum, to play. He played for about an hour without stopping, not even to have another can of Pabst Blue Ribbon beer, which he could easily take and drink with one hand while playing marvelous piano with the other. That night, he played every kind and style of piano you would ever want to hear. After that, Art figured we'd had enough. He called good night to everyone by playing *Little Man You've Had a Busy Day* which, without saying a word, meant that everybody had done his thing, all of those other players had played well but no one would play after him and he had played enough. Now it was time to go home.

When Tatum finished, everybody was exhausted from his gorgeous performance. Art was my number one favorite artist of all time and probably the greatest single musician that I have ever known.

I don't think anybody admired Art more than Eddie Beal, a local pianist who tried to emulate him. Eddie was one of the group of musicians whose favorite brew was Bourbon, usually Old Crow. Some of these Old Crow drinkers had wives who drank it, too, and these ladies were referred to among their acquaintances as "The Crowettes".

To finish telling about Evelyn and me, when I joined the Navy and had a place to live off base, she came to San Francisco to be with me and we started living together. When I had a leave, we went down to Ensenada, Mexico to do a little fishing. And while we were there, since they had no waiting period, we decided to go ahead and get married. We've been happily married ever since! At the time of our marriage, Evelyn already had two kids and we raised them. We never did have any children of our own. Evelyn was just the right person for me, and marrying her was one of the nicest things that ever happened to me.

In 1945, I was discharged from the Navy with the rank of First Class Petty Officer. All I wanted was to go back to Los Angeles and make a home for my family and to get about as far from the Navy as I could.

One of my first jobs was at Billy Berg's in Hollywood. Eddie Heywood's orchestra was playing an engagement there but a few of his men had been picked up for marijuana possession so he had to make some changes. I replaced Lem Davis in the band. Others in this fine little seven piece group were Vic Dickenson and Henry Coker on trombone; and Parr Jones on trumpet. The drummer was a little guy out of Brooklyn named Keg Purnell. Ernie Shepherd was on bass and Eddie was the pianist. Eddie was a good arranger and gave us written scores for all the tunes we did. The big favorite with the public at that time was his rendition of *Begin The Beguine*, which always got a big hand.

Eddie Heywood was a composer as well as an arranger. The instrumentation he preferred in his band was really unusual, having two trombones, one trumpet and only one saxophone plus the rhythm section, but it gave him the kind of sound he wanted and which the public enjoyed.

After Billy Berg's, we worked in a club for three weeks over the Christmas to New Year holiday of 1945 in the Little Tokyo area of Los Angeles. Then the group's next engagement was at the Three Deuces in New York City for a few months so I went East along with them.

Eddie was a very nervous person, very high strung, and he stuttered extensively but he was a nice guy and all he wanted was for the fellows to play good music. In fact, all the men really were fine musicians so I enjoyed being with him. Playing with a band that was well received made the working hours seem shorter.

While we were at the Three Deuces, a lot of big name musicians were playing alongside us on 52nd Street; people like Art Tatum and Dizzy Gillespie. It was an exciting time in New York and it gave Art and me a good chance to renew our friendship.

I only played with Eddie until the conclusion of the Three Deuces engagement in April 1946. Then I came back home and stayed in Los Angeles for the next four or five years because I didn't want to move, didn't want to be on the road, didn't want to go anywhere. I jobbed around, worked at the studios, did recordings and made a pretty nice living just staying in the city.

I recall that the Count Basie band came to town along about 1949 and they were playing a club out in South Los Angeles. I went down and sat in with the band, played the book on sight, tune after tune. Count got the idea then that he'd like to have me with his band, and asked me to join him at my convenience. But at that time I had no intention of going on the road. I was doing better than anyone in his band, just free-lancing, and had just bought myself a brand new car for cash. It was lucky for me that I wasn't tempted, because his big band broke up a couple of months later!

Typical of the sort of work that came in for me during those years was playing lead saxophone and contractor for Phil Moore. He was the music director for Discovery records. They decided to bring out some Lena Horne albums, using a 35-piece orchestra.

I also worked for the Phil Moore Four and One More. The four were the rhythm section and I was the one more, playing clarinet. Then it was decided to add a trumpet, making this a six piece group. The trumpet player was my brother Ernie, who had just returned from Europe.

After his discharge from the Navy, my brother received a telephone call from Duke Ellington inviting him to join his orchestra. Duke was looking for a trumpet replacement to take along on a European tour. It seems that one of his trumpet players, Al Killian, was being difficult. He was making some kind of demand, to be featured more or for more money or something, which Duke didn't want to go along with.

Ernie asked me "Should I go?" and I advised him that he should. I told him to get the experience, and that he could have himself a trip to Europe, see what the world was all about and have some fun, too. So Ernie went on the tour with Ellington to Europe. While he was playing with Duke in Paris, he met many people including Jacques Helian, who had a studio band there.

After that Ellington tour, Ernie returned to Los Angeles and joined me with the Phil Moore group. Irving Ashby was on guitar, Phil Moore on piano, and various other people were with us for a time. Ernie and I were the two horns, making this the Phil Moore Four Plus Two. We were working at a little place near Sunset and Vine, playing up a storm, when one night in walked Woody Herman. After we'd only played about one number, Woody started flipping. He got very excited and he said to me "I've got to get this guy," pointing to Ernie. He asked me who the trumpet player was and I answered "that's my kid brother."

Herman asked me if I would explain to Ernie what an advantage it would be to be for him to go with the Herman band.

I answered "I don't know what the advantage would be. He'd probably get good exposure being with you and," I added, "if you want to call that an advantage, most probably he'd be the only colored guy in the band."

Ernie accepted Woody Herman's offer at that time and joined his band. He did many tours with him and I was happy to hear that he did not have any racial troubles. Ernie was a tall, good-looking, light-skinned man and I suppose people seeing him with the rest of the white fellows in the Herman group just assumed that he had a white father. He really enjoyed playing with the Second Herd, the so-called Four Brothers band when the four saxes were featured. Ernie can be heard on trumpet on the phonograph records made at that time.

Ernie stayed with Herman for a while but left to take Maynard Ferguson's place in Stan Kenton's orchestra, playing those high notes. He told me it was "quite an experience to be with a band that played that loud." While he was with Kenton, Jacques Helian, whom he'd met while on tour with Ellington, called him to come to work in France. Ernie agreed, went to Paris and stayed there for a couple of years with his family.

In 1945, Ernie and his wife had a son who they named Ernie, Jr. Seemingly, my brother was very fond of the boy, very proud of him. When he went to live in France working with Jacques Helian, he took along his wife and son and they all lived there very happily. They lived the French way sending their boy to French schools and all. Ernie was easy to get along with and well-liked by the French people.

I watched over Ernie's little family, mostly from a distance. I was disappointed that, as Ernie Jr grew older, he wasn't closer to his father. I always thought that for a boy growing up, much of the influence should come from the father's side as it had been for us. In our home, my father was the most important person and in my eyesight, the father should be predominant. Although I loved my mother intensely, I admired my father enormously and I tried to emulate him in every way. In Ernie's family, it seemed as if the boy was not raised as a Royal; he was a Duseau, his mother's son.

It was a disappointment to me that Ernie didn't have more time to spend with the boy as he was growing up. I know that my brother worked very long hours during the day and by the time he came home at night, he was pretty tired. As a result, he didn't have much time to spend with his boy. But I don't think Ernie was disappointed. When Ernie Jr. grew up, he went to the New York Institute of Technology and came out with a diploma. He's doing very well these days as a CPA or some such profession. He made my brother Ernie extremely happy when he married and made my brother a grandfather by having a son, Jason, and couple of daughters.

When Ernie came back from France, he and the family settled in the New York area. I think Ernie was always contented living and working on the East Coast, while I remained a strictly West Coast musician. Very seldom do I ever get to New York, excepting on business, and that city has gotten to be pretty big for me.

Although I worked with my brother Ernie many, many times over these long intervening years, making individual recordings with various groups, that engagement with Phil Moore in Hollywood was the last time we ever played together in an organized band.

Meanwhile, I was still freelancing and always active in the Musicians' Union. My father had been Union president when I was a child and I was carrying on the family tradition by being

1 Marshal Royal Senior, 1919.

2 The Three Royals Orchestra: Ernestine Royal (piano), Marshal Royal Sr. (banjo), Ernest Royal (alto sax).

3 Royal Community Orchestra, around 1914, Sapulpa, Oklahoma. Marshal Jr. is "band mascot" in the middle of the front row.

5 Ernestine Royal with baby Ernie at three weeks.

6 Marshal Royal Jr. at about one year.

7 Curtis Mosby's Blue Blowers, 1930–31, Apex Nightclub, San Francisco.

8 Les Hite Orchestra at the Warner Bros. studios, 1931–32.

9 Les Hite Orchestra, 1934. Marshal is immediately to the right of Hite.

10 The full cast at Frank Sebastian's New Cotton Club, Culver City, California, early 1930s. Marshal is at the extreme right.

11 His Master's Voice: Petty Officer (First Class) Marshal Royal and his wire-haired terrier "Mike".

12 Marshal directs the St. Mary's Pre-flight Orchestra at Mare Island Navy Base.

13 Marshal fronting the Pre-flight Orchestra, 1944.

14 Marshal (clarinet) with Lionel Hampton (vibes) 1941–42.

15 Marshal solos with Lionel Hampton's Orchestra.

16 Marshal and Evelyn Royal, 1944.

17 Ernie and Flo Royal with Ernie Jr. in
Paris, late 1940s.

18 Ernie Royal.

19 Marshal and that naval cap adopted
by Basie.

20 Marshal with Count Basie, early 1960s.

21 The Basie Orchestra relax with Frank Sinatra and Quincy Jones, 1968.

22 All-star tribute to Duke Ellington. Marshal (third saxophone from right) sits next to Ellington sax-player Russell Procope (second from right) backing Sarah Vaughan, Sammy Davis Jr., Peggy Lee, Paula Kelly and Joe Williams.

active in the Union, too. I served on the board of directors of Local 767 from the time I was twenty-one years old. I was a part of what was going on, doing the best possible with what was happening in our area.

I got to know a fellow named Elmer Fain when I was just getting started working at the Musicians' Union. He was a business representative, a walking delegate for Local 767. At one time he was an alto sax player, but not anything like being a great musician. He was much in demand for the kind of movie where you'd see some Afro-American people running through the jungles with breech cloths on and holding spears and that sort of thing. He was a large, very dark-complected man and made a great deal of his income from doing that sort of movie work. In this day, it would be called quite degrading for people of color. But in those days you had to do what was necessary to make a living. And Fain really knew how to do it.

One of his great attributes was that he knew how to get jobs. He could walk into a place where the owner had no intention of hiring any musicians or having any live entertainment at all. Before he could realize what was going on, Fain had the owner convinced that he should put in some type of instrumentation. Elmer was always a great provider of jobs for the local musicians who needed work. There aren't enough men doing that sort of job any more. Just recently, February 1990, Elmer Fain was buried. I respected the man,and I was very sorry to see him go. I know he will be missed by a lot of people.

Over the years at different times, we tried to get the two Unions together. By 1950, there was more of an affirmative action feeling, which actually led to the meeting of the minds of the two Musicians' Unions. In 1950, just before I went with Basie, my old friend Leo Davis was president of the black Musicians' Union, 767, and I was vice-president. When I decided to leave town, I had to give up my position and let them appoint someone else as vice-president. The person appointed was Bill Douglas who today is treasurer of Local 47 The amalgamation of the two Unions that we had worked for happened shortly after I went to work for Basie.

8
With Count Basie

Yes, after all those years in the Los Angeles area, I finally decided I was ready for a change of scenery. Count Basie called me to join him toward the end of 1950. It was just after Christmas, as I recall. When I agreed, I only intended to stay out for three or four months but ended up staying with him for twenty years!

At the time, Count had an exciting seven piece group including Clark Terry on trumpet. Although Basie had asked me to join the big band on other occasions, this particular time it may have been because of Clark's recommendation that Basie decided to call me to work with the small group. I first met Clark at the Great Lakes Naval Station when we were both in the Navy waiting for reassignment. We became close friends and later ran into each other again when I was working on the East Coast with Eddie Heywood.

When I joined Count, I took Buddy DeFranco's place playing clarinet. Buddy left Basie with the intention of starting a band of his own but it didn't turn out that way. To be factual, I did not take Buddy's place because nobody ever really takes anybody else's place. You just fill a vacancy. Buddy was a good player and he still is. At any rate, I was hired to play clarinet with the seven piece group. Even though I had my saxophone with me, I maybe played only one or two tunes on it during the course of an evening and sometimes not at all.

Others in that band were Clark Terry on trumpet and Wardell Gray, who was the third horn, playing tenor sax. Both of these men were not just good, they were giants on their particular instruments. In the rhythm section, Gus Johnson was the drummer. He was one of the guys who kept just immaculate rhythm then and he still can, even today, 35 or 40 years later! He was probably as good a "time" drummer as Basie ever had and I liked the man personally. We had a lot of fun together.

Jimmy Lewis played the bass when I joined the Basie group. He was a flashy, very handsome, very dark complected man with an infectious smile. He played good acoustic bass and did the job excellently although he was partially self-taught.

There was also the perennial Freddie Green on guitar. Freddie had been with Basie since the Lord formed the world, it seemed like. He was with the band from 1937 until he died just a couple of years ago. He never played electric guitar, always just straight acoustic guitar and he was the best that ever did it. Hundreds of people throughout this world have tried to attain the particular sound, the drive, the rhythmic patterns of Freddie Green but no one has ever really got to the place where they played that particular type of guitar as well. It wouldn't be too productive these days, though, because it isn't loud enough, according to how loudly bands seem to play lately. Freddie Green never left the Basie band until the day that he died. He came home from work in Las Vegas one morning, had a heart attack and that was it.

The important man in our seven-piece group was Basie on piano. We had a lot of fun playing together. For me, it was a very good experience working with the seven piece band because we had no written music, everything was off the top of the head. Sometimes, by experimentation, we could really get into things that we had never gotten into before. Playing with Basie then was one of the happiest times I ever had, playing what we wanted, the way we wanted, and when we wanted. After the big Basie band was formed, Count always tried to keep together this nucleus from this small group.

The big Basie band of the fifties actually evolved from this seven piece combo. We were in New York when Basie was urged by his manager, Willard Alexander, to form a big band quickly. Alexander had us booked as a big band to play an engagement in a couple of weeks at the Strand Theater in New York City, at Broadway and 46th. Basie was to form this big band and work with a prominent vocalist who would be headlined. Offhand, I'm not sure if this was Billie Holiday or Ella Fitzgerald but I think it was Ella who was the top performer on the bill for that particular engagement. We also carried a comedian as part of the show, Big Time Crip, a one legged dancer, who opened up the program for us. He had a good act and got us off to a fine start.

The group we got together was a New York pick-up band, bringing many strangers together. Basie engaged a whole lot of fellows who were popular around the East Coast area, all first-rate musicians. We added Lucky Thompson on tenor sax. This was Lucky's second time in the Basie band. I remember meeting him at the Orpheum Theater in Los Angeles when he was playing with the Basie band in the late 30s or early 40s. Lucky was always a great tenor player but seemingly he wanted to be a band leader on his own, have his own group. He really wasn't too comfortable being a sideman. Or maybe it was that he preferred not being on the road, just wanted to stay in one place. I know at one time, he planned to stay out in the Los Angeles area and later wanted to remain around New York. This second time with Basie, he didn't stay too long, either, although he was well appreciated.

The other tenor sax was Wardell Gray, who was a true professional, one of the best. He had worked all around the country as a reputable young saxophone player, played with the Basie small group and stayed on in this new big band. Wardell was a little, slightly built man. Besides being very original in his style on the sax, he was a good composer as well. Some of his be-bop things which were recorded by Annie Ross were a very big help to the band. He was a very nice guy, quiet, and never harmed anybody in the world excepting himself.

We picked up Charlie Fowlkes on the baritone saxophone. Charlie was born in New York, or I should say, actually he was a Brooklynite; a real city boy. The first time we went on the road and into the South was the first time he'd ever seen cotton growing. He asked me what that was and I'd tell him they were marshmallow bushes. For a while he actually believed me! Earlier, two or three years before that, I heard that he'd been on the road with Tiny Bradshaw's orchestra and that was the first time he'd ever seen a live cow!

Charlie played a very good baritone sax. It's a big instru-ment and he was a big fellow to match, about six foot four, 290 pounds. We used to kid him sometimes and call him a great big goof, because of his size, but he was a big, lovable puppy and a lot of fun. He was also a wonderful guy and really a staunch friend of mine. I always enjoyed him being there.

Starting out, the other saxophonist was Bernie Peacock on alto and I, of course, took over as the leader of the section. But Bernie Peacock had some kind of problem. He left the band and was replaced by Ernie Wilkins. Ernie happened to have been a friend of Clark Terry's going back to their St. Louis days and he was also in the Navy during World War II. It was lucky for us that he came into the band at that particular time. He was one of the saviors of that 1951 Basie big band during its early days. Ernie made some new arrangements, put together the work we had been doing with the seven-piece band and added a lot of his own originals. His arrangements, along with the few we salvaged from Basie's old books, were about all we had to start with.

Ernie was a little guy, weighed about 135 pounds, and was a quiet fellow, a real introvert, never had much to say. For his size, he could consume as much beer as anybody in the world. He would sit down to write an arrangement and kill a case of beer in the process, without even getting up to go to the bathroom! Ernie was very kind, was and still is a nice man. I've always liked him a lot. He's still a great writer, one of the best there ever was, especially for big bands.

For the new band, Basie hired a whole lot of New York trumpet players. Mainly the section was built solidly around two men. Clark Terry stayed on. He was a strong person in the section, and always a stand-out. The other important trumpet man was Al Porcino, an Italian fellow, a very good player, and part of the time he played lead trumpet.

One of the trombones was another New Yorker, Matthew Gee. He was originally from somewhere in the south, Houston, Texas or somewhere thereabouts, but he suddenly turned out to be a New Yorker. A lot of guys who consider themselves to be musicians, once they got to New York wouldn't leave there even to go to heaven. He was one of those guys. Once he got to the Big Apple, he just stayed around there. He was good in the bebop style with a pretty nice tone. Unfortunately, he was another fellow with the chemical problems and is no longer with us.

We played that particular engagement with the big band to great success, which convinced Willard Alexander that he should persuade Basie to keep the big band. Now big bands were in a very, very sad state at that time. Financially, they just couldn't make it. They couldn't earn enough money to pay to keep a big band on the road.

Shortly after we went out on the road, we did lose some of the old guard. Jimmy Lewis, our first-rate bass player, didn't want to leave New York. It was necessary for him to stay in town and I think the reason was that he wanted to be near his wife. Later he wound up as one of the most sought after electric bass players around New York, among the rock and roll set.

We were doing one-nighters, traveling in charter buses throughout the east and trying to build up a listing of dates to play. Many times the band was paid as little as $500 a night for the whole seventeen pieces along with a band valet, the bus charter and all the rest of the expenses. This was very hard to manage. We had some hard, hard times trying to keep the big band together. The money wasn't good and there were many sacrifices in that band. We struggled along with that kind of burden for a year or so.

Basie wasn't lenient with his dollars, with the pay checks, but the fact was that he didn't really have much to throw around. For the first year or two he lost a lot of money with the big band because of these financial handicaps.

For the musicians, being on the road when you are not paid well is a real sacrifice. It costs musicians double to maintain a home base while paying for hotel rooms and restaurant meals on the road. We traveled somewhere almost every night and always had to pay all our own bills. In the 20 years I was with him, Basie never picked up my food nor hotel bill, at any time, under any circumstances.

But having said that, let me mention one outstanding trip which took place around the last month or so of my being with the band. This would have been the winter of 1969. At the time, the Basie band was at one of its highest levels so far as acceptance and popularity among the people who listened to this type of jazz.

That is probably why the orchestra was selected to play for a jazz tour on the Cunard Line's *Queen Elizabeth II*. For several previous years she had only sailed from New York to London and back. This particular trip was launching the QE2's first Caribbean cruise.

One of the nicest thing about the trip is that the deal allowed me to bring my wife, Evelyn, along on the cruise, too. When Evelyn and I left New York for the Caribbean, it was the dead of winter and snowing so we were looking forward to the warmer weather. On the QE2, we had excellent accommodation. This ship was, and probably still is, one of the finest luxury liners on the water. When we got to Cape Hatteras, sometimes described as being the graveyard of certain ships, we encountered one of the severest storms you could imagine. I don't know the exact tonnage of the QE2, but from all indications, it was too small for the elements of nature. The storm and the high seas of Cape Hatteras almost turned that large ship upside down a few times!

The Basie band was not required to play every day as a part of the ship's schedule but we wouldn't have been able to play that day, or for the next two either because everybody was sick, even the captain of the ship! Sick bay was overflowing with people trying to get something to counteract their seasickness.

About a day or so out of Cape Hatteras, the seas calmed down and the weather turned beautiful. We visited several ports in the Caribbean and everything was just gorgeous. We only played about three times during the twelve day voyage but we were a great success and treated just splendidly. Everyone seemed to take us into their hearts. It was as though we were wealthy, paying customers on the ship, not just hired help. The whole band was included in the better-class seating for all meals, with the best of facilities and a couple of times we were invited to be guests of the high-ranking officers at their tables. I have never been better treated for food and all the niceties that usually only come to the very rich. I always look back and think well of Basie for having provided me with such a beautiful vacation, under pleasant working conditions and in the company of my wife. We were treated just royally, to coin a phrase out of my name.

Back in the early fifties during the rough period, we lost many of the New York contingent of musicians and had to pick up others along the way. Some of the regular musicians had little chemical dependencies, and you can't run a successful band with that kind of fellow. Basie always insisted on having a clean band. So there were a lot of changes. Not all these were caused by this type of problem, though. There were also incompatibilities between certain people in the sections as will happen among a group of musicians.

Also, during the fifties, things were not that good on the road. I'm speaking about accommodations. Conditions were still pretty bad and the Basie band traveled strictly second class. None of the white hotels were open for black artists. This was one hundred per cent true in the South and ninety percent in the near South. You couldn't stay in the nice hotels. We usually had friends who recommended us to different homes and by this time, there were a few hotels owned by blacks. On the West Coast there were a few Japanese hotels where we could stay and which didn't adhere to the jim crow policies. But it was usually second class hotel bookings all the way.

The change came gradually in the South after the Martin Luther King era. Then, acceptance there was tongue-in-cheek and even in the North, prejudice never totally disappeared. Even today! Compliance, the way they have it in the North, sometimes can be as bad or worse than all-out prejudice, because with all-out prejudice you know where you stand. The way things are in the North, a black will always be a black and a white will always be a white, just as it has been for hundreds of years.

Even in Las Vegas in the fifties, some of our greatest entertainers, some of the top black women stars, could not stay inside the hotels where they were working! There'd be a trailer in the yard outside of the hotel which would be their dressing room and where they'd sleep.

I know this at first hand because the Basie band was hired to play one of the show rooms in Las Vegas in late 1951 and early '52. I think we were not only the first big band to work a show room but also the first black band to play in any of the big show rooms.

At one time, I have the impression that Pearl Bailey was on the bill with us. I do know she was in Vegas at the same time and we were all living in the same little motel "behind the iron curtain" as we used to call it, where practically all the black entertainers in town stayed. Yes, there was a little ghetto area there. Las Vegas was not the South, but that doesn't mean that the black brethren could go and do what they wanted to do, either.

Las Vegas then was just as segregated as the South at its worst. We stayed in a place called Mrs. Shaw's Motel, which bore absolutely no resemblance to any decent motel I've ever seen. That place was nearly as bad as the Gem Hotel in Fort Worth, Texas. There was one tree in the yard, which was the only shade anywhere around. Basie, I and a few other people all tried to get up early enough to go outside and get under that one tree, where we could get a little relief from the sun. We'd listen to the portable radio we had and the Las Vegas announcer would say something like, "its raining out here on the strip and people are running out of the pool to get inside." This was utterly ridiculous. We were quite close to the Strip and there was nothing but dust where we were staying or as far as we could see out in that direction.

We brought out the same show to Las Vegas that we'd done in New York; chorus girls and everything. Besides the chorus line, we had Redd Foxx and Bill Bailey, Pearl Bailey's brother, appearing with us, too. We were a big success. Although we had struggled to make ends meet, by the same token, we opened up a lot of avenues for black big bands when we played those big rooms in Las Vegas. As everybody knows, that's where a whole lot of money changes hands.

We also appeared a time or two on the same bill with Frank Sinatra, who was at the height of his popularity, around that time. The ads would simply read "Sinatra's back in town." Everything lit up on the Strip. Quincy Jones, who was his musical director, later did an album with the Basie band.

We spent a lot of time traveling in the bus. For amusement, the fellows had what we called the Bat Club. A "bat" was an ugly lady. She could be a nice girl, pure of heart, but if she was homely, she was a Bat. Any time one of the guys in the band was caught by another fellow sneaking off with a Bat or taking one to his room, he was immediately penalized. As soon as we got back on the bus, we had a judge, a Bat Club jury and so on. We would levy a monetary fine on the person caught with a Bat. It cost a fellow five dollars on up, depending on the particular Bat he was caught with or if it was a repeat performance. That was the Basie Bat Club.

When a band goes out on the road, the men always are on the lookout for the ladies. Being away from home, it's no strange thing. The interesting part is that the girls were looking for us, too! The ones who hung around the bandstand back in the old days were the first groupies, the band girls of the road. These girls were music lovers who wanted to make it with the guys and most of the times, the guys were quite willing.

Some fellows had a terrific way with the ladies and I can't think of anybody who was more elegant and eloquent than Duke Ellington. With his line, he had a bevy of beauties everywhere. Sometimes when the ladies would see me, they'd say "You look a lot like Ellington. You remind me a lot of Duke." Gradually I'd come to realize that the ladies had turned things around and were making a hit on me!

Traveling on the road such as we did with Basie, we stayed out sometimes as much as fifty weeks a year. When I say "on the road", I mean away from home. Practically everywhere in the world was away from home for me, because I am a West Coast musician. Being with ten or fifteen fellows on a constant basis, you find out that there are really some strange guys in the band. One of the most hated guys in *any* band is the kind of fellow who calls home to either his girl friend or his wife and tells her exactly what everybody in the band has been doing for the past week. He tells her who they slept with, who they had dinner with, who they had drinks with, and so on in detail. As soon as this fellow hangs up, she is on the phone calling the wife or girl friend of the fellows she's heard secrets about and telling them what she heard. Then, when the musician came back to town, his wife or girlfriend knew all the details of what he had been doing, with names. In several cases, it caused break-ups or near break-ups in these people's

94

lives.

Our drummer Gus Johnson left the band, but not under ordinary circumstances. I don't know whether it was his appendix or what, but he took sick and had to go to the hospital for an operation of some kind. During that time, Basie experimented with many drummers around but none of them really cut it.

By chance I helped to find a replacement drummer. We were in New York City and Sarah Vaughan and I had just left an after-hour session early one morning. It was about seven and we were walking back toward the hotel. As we walked, it was turning daylight when we spotted this little guy coming by in his automobile. I recognized him from having seen him on the Larry Steele show in Atlantic City. It was Sonny Payne, who was on his way to work in a factory where he was doing hard labor. I waved for him to stop and I told him about our troubles finding a satisfactory drummer. I said to him, "I would like for you to get in touch with Basie and see if you can't come out and play a night or two with us."

Well, Sonny got in touch with Basie and came out and worked with us. Sonny really knew his drums. He was the step-son of Chris Columbus, a drummer who worked with the Wild Bill Davis Trio. Basie took to Sonny and could see that, with a little bit of tutoring, he could be a damn good drummer, so he was hired to join us. Not too much later, Gus Johnson recovered from his surgery and was ready to return, but Basie didn't hire him back. He decided to keep Sonny, instead. At that time, it became a running joke, "if you ever get sick in Basie's band, when you want to come back there won't be a job for you."

Later on, that same thing happened with Charlie Fowlkes. He was up on a ladder hanging Christmas decorations when he fell off and broke his ankle. He couldn't come in to work so Eddie "Lockjaw" Davis recommended another baritone saxophone player as a replacement. Lockjaw at that time was manoeuvring around to be road manager. He wanted to be Mr. Big with the Basie band and anybody he couldn't control was on his get-rid-of list. Those days, Lockjaw was making pretty strong recommendations to Basie and Basie was listening. Too bad for Charlie

Fowlkes that he was one of the people Lockjaw could not control. So when he recommended this guy, Cecil Payne, he was hired and he stayed. He was a big, strong, quiet dude, and a very good baritone player.

The end of the story is that Charlie Fowlkes was let out of the band when he was sick, lying flat on his back and couldn't speak up on his own behalf. After it had happened twice, it wasn't a joke anymore, it became like a warning slogan with the fellows, "don't ever get sick in the Basie's band, because when you're ready to come back, there won't be a job for you!"

There were other changes during those years. Wardell Gray left, he wanted to do his own thing, and Paul Quinichette joined us. We were still adjusting from the seven-piece band to the big group. I knew Paul from having seen him in Los Angeles. At that time he was having a little problem with his chemicals as well as with alcohol. He begged me to intercede for him and help him get a regular job with the Basie band. John Hammond, who was always a man who put himself in front and helped people to get started in jazz, made several albums as director along with Paul Quinichette. I spoke with Basie, Paul joined us and he stayed for about a year. He left along with the good tidings of John Hammond, who was one of Basie's top fans. As for Wardell, many years later and quite a while after he left the Basie band, he was in the Las Vegas area. This was mixed up some way with his chemical problems and he was found dead in the desert. To this day nobody knows exactly what happened or how he died.

You usually think about trumpets and tenor saxophones when you think about solos in the Basie band. But one of the unsung players for many years was a trombonist I recommended to Basie somewhere back in about 1952. Henry Coker was originally from Texas but had lived in Hawaii and the West Coast for years, where I think he played with Benny Carter. He was immediately installed as a lead player as soon as he came into the Basie band. He was a very good trombone player and played good jazz solos in his own distinctive style. Henry Coker was a real original.

Al Grey was another trombone player who joined Basie. He

came out of Dizzy Gillespie's band and before that, he had played with Lionel Hampton. During the time he was with Basie, Al developed into a very good manipulator of the plunger. This is a rubber instrument, just like the household item which is used for plumbing repairs. Both trumpets and trombones use the plunger to make a wah-wah or other sound. So Al Grey was often referred to as "the last of the big plungers."

We kept moving and when we got back in the Chicago area, Basie picked up a "boy singer" who proved to be a life saver for the band. Now, the term "boy singer" does not refer to the singer's age, whether's he's young or not. It used to be the common expression for the male singer with a band. That "boy singer" was Joe Williams.

Joe joined us in late 1954 or early 1955. Earlier, he had occasionally worked with Basie's smaller band around the Chicago area. As we came through Chicago, Joe was still there and not exactly at the top of his career. It was Reunald Jones, the trumpet player, who persuaded Joe to come down and do a couple of songs with us while we were playing a gig on the South Side of Chicago. He did, Basie took to him again and hired him to go out on the road with us. In my opinion, this was one of the best moves that Basie ever made.

When Joe joined us, he had no music, no arrangements, no nothing except just that big, wonderful, fabulous voice, which he really knew how to use. For a few months, he was mostly stuck with the repertoire of Basie's former vocalist, "Mr.Five By Five" Jimmy Rushing, because those were the arrangements in our book. Joe had been with the old big band years before and we still had a couple of his arrangements. Joe also sang some of his own choices of tunes and we quickly put head arrangements together for him.

After Joe had been with us for a while, Frank Foster and Ernie Wilkins were mainly responsible for writing some new arrangements for the whole big band which would be appropriate for Joe or anybody else. Foster was a genius at putting together good-sounding arrangements for a vocalist and Ernie did a few things like *Every Day I Have the Blues* and the perennial favorite

All Right, Okay, You Win. In no time, Joe became an enormous and important part of the Basie band as a vocalist.

While this was actually very good for Basie, it was a twist of fate for him. He had told me personally that never in his life would he ever let another band vocalist get to be as important a personage as Jimmy Rushing had become while he was with the Basie band. Now, all that was kicked aside. Shortly after Joe Williams joined us, we made some records with him that turned out to be big hits. Joe got to be a popular star and more capable of handling himself than anybody Basie had ever had singing for him before. I'm happy to say this about Joe because he is a fine man and still one of my favorite people today.

Joe Williams and Count Basie turned out to be a terrific combination, with a string of big sellers. Next time we came into Birdland in New York, we were all the rage. It got to the point that Basie was so popular that the Birdland ads would simply read "BASIE'S BACK," with no name, just Birdland's address under it. That was enough! The whole town came out to hear us. Fancy automobiles would be parked three deep. I mean Cadillacs, Mercedes, Rolls Royces and what have you, parked for the whole block between 52nd and 53rd Streets on one side of the street. People stood in line to get in to hear the Basie band!

9
The Birdland Years

The Basie band deserved all the attention it got at that time. It really was a good band. I rehearsed that band, took some things out and put them together, made them more playable and successful. That was my job. Being with a big band was my meat, what I enjoyed playing the most then and still do.

I've always felt very, very proud of the band. Though I didn't do any of the arranging, I felt that I had contributed something important to the band by rehearsing the men, helping to give the saxophone section its distinctive sound and so on. It happened very gradually that Count had come to lean on me. It was a thing that just happened over time. Nobody said "We're going to be a band and Marshal Royal, you're going to be the task master." It wasn't like that.

While I was with Basie, it was just that I'd be there, we'd run into something and he'd say "Hey, Marshal, what can we do over here?" or "What's wrong over there?"

And I'd tell him what was wrong. Sometimes we'd get together and Basie would say something like "From now on, you will be doing this."

And even when he didn't, I'd take over where I thought I could be useful.

Working in a band, if you and the leader like each other and you get along well together, you do things for him. Then, you don't work *for* your band leader, you work *with* your leader. That's the difference. Most people work for the leader, which I think is entirely wrong. To me, that's just the same as going out, getting a pick and shovel and working for the city breaking gravel or some other menial job. But if you are working for and with, at the same time, then it's a different story. That's the way it was with Basie and me so I was pleased to be sort of a straw boss for him.

We fellows in the Basie band were together like a group of brothers. When we started an engagement, all the men were on the stand, ready to go. We were not just a collection of individual musicians. With the downbeat, it was *wham!* and we were like a machine with all the parts working together. We could attribute a lot of our success to our being regimented and the best organized, best rehearsed band on the road.

Yet, about the only time that we had regular rehearsals was when we were sitting down in New York, at Birdland. Then, we would always designate one day a week for rehearsal. We'd rehearse from one or two in the afternoon until five or six in the evening, but that was just the fellows in the band, without Basie or a piano player. Basie would be in the back of the room, trying to find out what horse was running at Aqueduct or some other racetrack. Later, when we were working for an audience, he'd be there playing our new things and everything would sound terrific. We'd get a stack of new music put in the books by the end of our New York stay.

When we were on the road, we'd bring out our own things. The first set of a dance night, we'd have a whole lot of new tunes and play them. Sometimes they sounded good, but usually we'd chop them up, take out the bad parts, play the good and keep on going. We'd change the tempos and put it where it felt right. Doing one-nighters, the band learned the arrangements through playing them over and over, and that was the extent of our rehearsals.

The most important thing with rehearsing a band, I've found, is to try to keep people happy and from hurting their musical intuition, because jazz music has its own form, which comes about through individual performances. I always had my own way of rehearsing different groups. I believe in "passive persuasion," which means that you show people what you want to be done without actually letting them know that they are being shown and without arguing with anyone. That takes out the element of personal embarrassment. You get more achieved by letting the men think they are the ones who are actually the innovators. Every man can have his own likes and dislikes. You'll probably never find two guys with exactly the same tastes. The main thing in rehearsals is having mutual respect, and if the side

100

men have respect for you, then you'll get the job done. If they don't, it's no good, because it won't work. If you can command enough respect in front of a group, then it works out fine.

Getting guys to tune up is probably the worst problem, because any time you tell a fellow he is not in tune, he is likely to look up and ask you, "How do you know that? How do you know I am out of tune?" There is no answer to that except it is your opinion against his. If you can get everybody tuned up at the same time at the same pitch, regardless of how you get it done, even if everyone is out of tune it's like getting a complete band to make a mistake at the same time. It becomes right because everyone is doing it together.

The fellows in the band called Basie "the Chief" and I was called the Burgermeister because I was the music director, in charge of a whole lot of the rehearsing of that fifties band. Before joining Basie, I never had a nickname and that was the only time in my entire career that I ever had one.

After I first got out of the Navy, a photographer who was entering some sort of competition posed me for a couple of mood shots. He liked the way the shadows from the yachting cap hit my face. I'd often worn one, starting in 1934 when I rented a convertible. Basie saw the cap, liked it a lot and took to wearing one himself. In later years, you hardly saw him without it.

Count Basie was an amiable man and he had a pretty good way of getting along with his men. He did have one quirk, though. For years, he'd keep a fifth of Johnny Walker Red under his piano just for himself and wouldn't hardly give anybody a taste. He always drank a strong whiskey and used to say that he couldn't stand a wine drinker. There probably never was any fellow who was a wine drinker in the band so I don't know who he was referring to, but he made that statement many times.

Basie always knew how to keep his band together and work them. It was strange, though, how he'd pit two different people against one another to keep things going. He was one of the first band leaders to start two tenors battling each other. It would get so they didn't even like each other too much, which seemed to act as an incentive for them to keep trying to outdo the other fellow.

It motivated them to play better, so his little scheme worked. Other than that, he got along well with the men in his band.

Contrast that to the Ellington band. Sometimes Duke would start a set with only seven men on the stage out of a seventeen-piece band and he would go on like nothing was wrong. But when the men got back on the band stand, if someone had been drinking, the next tune would feature *him*, so that fellow would fall on his face and make a fool of himself. With the Basie band, it was different. There was no such thing as trying to make a man look foolish or turning your back on someone for six or eight months without speaking to him.

Another difference is that in the Basie band, it was not necessarily decided in advance who was to have the solos on a piece. Most arrangements were not written around a particular man with the idea that he'd do the solo. If the solo happened to come along during rehearsal and a guy was playing, if he was a good solo player and wanted to keep it, he kept it.

One of our champion soloists was our drummer, Sonny Payne. He was probably one of the better showmen of all time as far as his drumming went. He got to the place where he could practically do his own act. We'd be playing a particular tune, *Old Man River*. Then, the whole band would walk off the band stand. We'd go out and take a smoke, stay off for five or ten minutes before we would come back, during which time Sonny Payne would be doing his act, playing his different rhythms along with shoveling his sticks from hand to hand, and all the things that made entertainment for the audience, who liked that sort of thing. He had a great act and most of us in that band had a very good relationship with him. But at times, Sonny was resented by some of the other fellows in the band who thought he was getting too much consideration and publicity out of his playing.

In fact, Sonny deserved every bit of attention he got because he was doing a great job. One of the main people who really didn't like Sonny was Lockjaw Davis. During the time Lockjaw was with the band, he tried to do little things to discourage and discredit Sonny because Lockjaw was the sort of self-centered man who liked to be out in front, himself, at all times. But Sonny could outmaneuver just about anybody in the band when it came to receiving acclaim and applause for what he was doing. Overall, he was probably as good as any drummer Basie ever had and better than most. In my opinion, Sonny never really received credit for all that he was.

Luckily for Basie, many of the fine musicians he hired to join the band also turned out to be great arrangers. Thad Jones was one of my all time favorite arrangers, along with Ernie Wilkins, Frank Wess and Frank Foster. Each contributed a huge amount to "the Basie sound." The original Basie band had mainly featured individual soloists but the new band of the early 50s was built on an ensemble playing band, a different sound from the regular type of band. The band was well rehearsed, and the fine arrangements that Ernie Wilkins, the two Franks and others wrote gave the new Basie band its individual, new sound.

Frank Wess was one of the "two Franks", as we used to call them. He was a tenor saxophone player out of Washington and one of the men who could also arrange. He was a very good stylist and I would consider him to be the forerunner of all the jazz flute players. There are others who played flute, of course, but in my opinion he was the first and the best of the jazz flute players.

Shortly after he joined us, another tenor sax man came into the band. This was Frank Foster, the other Frank, who was recommended, I believe, by Billy Eckstine. We'd done some tours with Billy and he told us about this talented young fellow from Ohio whose mother taught at Wilberforce College there. Billy had seen the young man while he was wearing a service uniform and I don't think he was even out of his teens yet.

Young Frank just loved to play and it got so you couldn't go anywhere after hours without finding Frank Foster there, jamming. Basie hired him to replace someone he had gotten fed up with. At the time, we didn't know what kind of writer he was. He turned out to be one of the best jazz arrangers in the business. And he still is about as good as you can find. He could double other instruments but mainly his instrument was and is tenor saxophone. Since Basie's death, he has taken over the leadership of the Count Basie Orchestra.

103

Shortly after Frank Foster came in, there was an addition to the band of a man who I consider one of the best arrangers I have ever known in my life. That was Thad Jones, who joined us on trumpet. He was a great trumpet player, one of three famous musical brothers: Hank Jones and Elvin Jones were the other two. Not one of those three ever had to take a back seat to anybody. Besides being a great trumpet player, I always considered Thad to be the modern day, next-generation Duke Ellington. This was demonstrated by his writing, his mannerisms and his method of exploiting musicians around him. Today, probably all writers and arrangers of good organized jazz orchestrations have listened at one time or another to Thad Jones. If he was still living, he'd be considered very important even today because you don't ever lose that kind of talent. He had it and could not be denied.

Ernie Wilkins was important in forming the big band in the early fifties. He was one of the best writers any man could ever have. He did many hits for Joe Williams and for the Basie band but never had the recognition that should have been given to him as a writer. I went out of my way to introduce Ernie to Tommy Dorsey during one of the times we were playing in the same town. I talked with Dorsey and told him about Ernie, which led to Dorsey's hiring him to make some arrangements for his band. It was only two, three or four at that time and then Ernie took sick and wasn't able to do more for Dorsey. He is one of the forgotten heroes in Basie's second big band; one of the people who helped him become a millionaire.

I always tried to encourage Basie to let each one of these fine sidemen-arrangers do his own album. Basie had a marvelous entourage of arrangers, Thad Jones, Frank Foster, Frank Wess, and Ernie Wilkins, the greatest array of wonderful musical jazz writers that any band in the business ever had. They even put Basie's name on some of their things and yet he never singled out any of these fellows to do his own complete album. Seemingly, the choice of tunes and albums was controlled by other people who were not really associated with the Basie band. And apparently there was also the politics of people like Teddy Reig, who was a staunch friend of Basie's as well as recording superviser for

Roulette records. It was a real disappointment to me that none of these fellows had his own album.

Over the years, there were other fine arrangers, men who were not in the band, doing charts for us such as Quincy Jones, Billy Byers, and at times, Nat Pierce. One of our most successful albums was arranged by Neal Hefti, a white writer. This was the album called simply *Basie*, which became one of our better-known efforts. Many of the tunes in the Basie version of Hefti's tunes were the very same ones which had been recorded previously by Hefti's own band. But his band had just keeled over and done nothing. By our changing the tempos on some of these catchy tunes, we wound up with a big winner. We had a way of changing tempos of other people's tunes to give them "the Basie band sound."

You could probably count the times on your fingers that Basie actually fired a man. He would usually allow a man enough rope to hang himself and then the fellow would just leave. But I remember one of the few times that Basie fired someone. Reunald Jones, the trumpet player, could get up on the bandstand and play his horn with one hand, his legs crossed and seldom miss anything. Basie let him go because Reunald was very adept at keeping up with the Union rules, the way that musicians should be treated, their pay, when extra pay was due and so on. He kept a ledger of those things and figured Basie had underpaid him. When we'd get into New York, he'd go down to the Union, Local 802. Then he'd ask Count why he hadn't received such and such an amount of money, which grated on Basie's feelings. Basie owed him, alright, but he hadn't done it deliberately. Reunald kept it up until Basie finally thought he was incorrigible and let him go.

After he left us, Lee Young called to tell me that the Nat Cole group was looking for a trumpet player to go on the road with them. At the time, Lee was drummer and music director, I believe, for King Cole and so when he asked me who I could recommend as trumpet player, I recommended Reunald Jones, who went with Nat and stayed with him for several years.

Basie hired Snooky Young to take Reunald Jones's chair. Snooky had been with the original big band many years before, then he had retired from the road. He went back to his home in Ohio and was working in some type of trade other than music and gigging on the side. Basie prevailed on Snooky to come back on the road and be a part of the band. It was about 1957 or so when Snooky came in and he remained with us until the sixties. He was always one of the better trumpet players and, with Basie, had a chance to show himself off. Snooky could play sweet tunes, leads, or take off on his horn in the modern style of that particular era. He was a lovable little guy, small, just a little over five feet tall. His real name was James, but the name Snooky went with his size and sweet personality and no one ever called him anything else.

He turned out to be another one of the natural assets of the Basie band, playing the leads throughout the years. After leaving Basie, he went with the *Tonight Show* band in New York City. Later, the *Tonight Show* moved to Los Angeles and so did Snooky. He was still with the show in 1990, living in Los Angeles, and managing to fit in a few jazz concerts and jazz parties. We have worked together from time to time on various entertainment ventures other than the *Tonight Show*.

We could look forward to playing at Birdland several times a year. In the summertime when we got to New York to play there, we had celebrations. One of these was the annual ball game. We'd form a softball team and play against the Birdland team. Morris Levy, who owned Birdland, helped out with their team by bringing in some ringers. He'd find a lot of young men like the leading softball pitcher for one of the teams, and get them in to play against the Basie team.

We had a pretty good team, though. Eddie Jones, the bass player, was a big fellow, who weighed about 280 pounds and looked like a back stop, so we made him the catcher. He had come to the Basie band straight out of Howard University, where he was a student and lineman on the football team. Eddie originally came from Red Bank, New Jersey and lived around the corner from the Basie family. He was very intelligent, read a book a day and always kept up his school training. He stayed with the Basie band for several years but left the music business and went into computer work some time ago. For the last ten years or so he has been setting up programs in Hartford, Connecticut, for one of the big insurance companies.

There wasn't anybody in the band who could pitch so we used to get Cat Anderson out of the Ellington band to be our pitcher. The rest of the band was strewn out at the various other places. We made Basie third base coach because even though Basie didn't know anything about softball, we had to put him someplace. It was his band and his team.

These games were a lot of fun. We always went up to the park at Bear Mountain, where we made reservations to use the soft ball diamond. We didn't have uniforms but we did have sweat shirts that said "Count Basie" on them. Morris Levy used to bring crates of fruits and vegetables, meat, all kinds of salads, cold cuts, cheeses, all the beer you could drink, hard liquor and even champagne, for the fellows who had a champagne taste. Well, that first year we knocked the soft ball pitcher out of the box by the second or third inning. Knocking him out of the box means that we made so many runs that we wore the pitcher out. We destroyed him. He had to keep throwing the ball so much we wore him out and they had to bring in a replacement. So we beat them.

About a year later, we came in again during the summer. That second year, Birdland had a young girl working in the check room whose husband was Joe Black, the pitcher for the Brooklyn Dodgers. They conscripted him to pitch against us. He wasn't allowed to pitch overhand, as he would have in a regular game. Instead, he had to pitch underhand for a soft ball game. We knocked him out of the box, too, in the third or fourth inning. We beat them so bad that the people who were managing the Birdland club, Oscar and Mrs. Goodstein, were standing in the corner with tears rolling down their faces. We'd put up a few bets and Birdland lost everything. That ended the softball game.

We thought we were pretty good and would like to have taken on another band with a good team. The Harry James band was supposed to have an excellent team, but we never got to play against them because we were never in the same city at the same time.

In its heyday, Birdland was "the place" and there was

always a line up of fancy cars out in front. Speaking of which, there was a time when occasionally a Rolls Royce came to pick me up. Back in 1945 when I was playing at Billy Berg's in Hollywood, I first got to know Ava Gardner. I was playing clarinet there with Eddie Heywood and she used to come into the club. She had been married at one time to Artie Shaw, liked the sound of a clarinet, so we got acquainted. Now, many years later with Basie, I saw her again. By then, she had been to Spain and had become fond of flamenco music. We were talking and I mentioned that I liked flamenco music, too. Ava asked me if I would like to go hear a very good Spanish group playing nearby, during my break. It happened that at Birdland, we used to get an hour and a quarter break around midnight. I told her that would be great and sure enough, she came by to get me in her Rolls.

Out in front of the canopy of Birdland is where all the hustlers and pimps and dope peddlers in New York would be hanging out. When I first came to the door and opened it with Ava Gardner beside me, their eyes were popping. We'd get into the Rolls Royce and go spend about an hour listening to the flamenco guitar player. Then we'd come back and Ava and I would get out of the Rolls and go back into Birdland. I must have made an immediate acquaintanceship with about ten or fifteen new "friends" who were planning to use me to try and meet Ava Gardner. They all wondered why in the hell she would be picking me up in her Rolls if we were just friends. But the fact is, that that's all we really were.

Morris Levy, who owned Birdland was a great guy and I had a lot of respect for him. He also owned Roulette Records and I recall being in his office and watching him do about three things at the same time. He'd be making a deal on the phone, adding up some figures on his desk and conducting another conversation, all at the same time. We were all sorry when Birdland closed.

10
More Basie Years

Gradually, the Basie band roamed further afield and we did European tours. Our first trip overseas was in 1954. We took the nucleus of the first big band and added a few people. Gus Johnson was still our drummer then. We added Joe Wilder on trumpet, and a girl singer named Bixie Crawford. She was not one of Basie's big, fat girl singers nor was she a youngster, either. Bixie was a mature woman when she came with us and at one time had been the singer with Louis Jordan and his Tympany Five. She was nice looking, had a good figure and stayed with the band a year or so. Before becoming a singer, she had gone to college and studied to be a teacher. In later years, she has taught school in Los Angeles.

When we arrived in Europe, we landed in Denmark first, then went to Sweden, Norway, the Netherlands and came on down through Germany, France and Switzerland. Nothing exciting happened in any of those places but when we got to England for the first time, we were thrown out of the hotel! The reason this happened is that there was a whole lot of partying going on after we played the concert. Some of the girls from the street, I don't mean fans, I mean hookers, started infiltrating the apartment hotel where we were staying.

When there seemed to be too much frivolity, it was reported to the manager and we were asked to leave the next day. That was the first, last and only time we had such an experience. It could have been avoided if it hadn't been for the English girls who came in looking for it to be financially rewarding for them and turned the evening from a celebration into a disturbance.

When we went to Europe for the first time and visited Scandinavia, we found out that the Danes sold all kinds of X-rated books and magazines, and these were sometimes so rancid they would be impounded by the U.S. Customs people when we came home. There was one particular fellow in the band who bought each and every paperback he could find and some eight and sixteen millimetre movies of pornographic shorts. He was able to bring back a lot of these books and magazines and movies, and the first person he showed all of them to was his mother!

The European audiences at that time were the greatest. It was clear that, for the European people, it was considered a wonderful treat to be able to view the Basie band in person and enjoy what we were playing. In the United States, jazz has always been a tongue-in-cheek project, just a throwaway kind of music. American people don't think of jazz as an art form and if they don't like it, they say to hell with it. Over there, we knew we could play and be appreciated.

In between concerts, I used to have a lot of fun with the children in the streets. While I would be eating in a restaurant, I'd look outside and see small smiling faces looking back at me through the window. They wanted my autograph which I was glad to give. Besides, I always had a pocketful of the little complimentary pieces of candy that were given to us to keep the ears from stopping up when the plane was landing. I'd save these to give to the little kids in the devastated German towns.

These places had been bombed by many, many planes during World War II and were still trying to get rebuilt, Mannheim, Stuttgart, Frankfurt, Bremen and so on. The little kids would be outside; some of them didn't even have proper clothing. The people of all the bombed countries over there worked 24 hours a day trying to improve their standard of living. Today, with the help of the Marshall Plan, it's practically all rebuilt, they're doing fine and it seems to me like they won the war, not the Allies.

While we were over there, we made some records. Sometimes we didn't know we were being recorded because the people were making these without anyone's permission. To be factual, I don't actually know how many times they were stealing and how many times Basie was aware that they were taping. I would spy speakers behind plants, in big flower pots and any place where you could conceal the equipment on the band stand. I'd report this to Basie as the leader, to the band manager or band boy; whoever was around. Sometimes the recording equipment would be removed and sometimes it would not. Over the years, it turned out that many records have been issued that I didn't know anything about and couldn't remember ever having recorded. Clearly, they were made on the scene while we were giving concerts.

Officially and to our knowledge, hardly any records were made at that time. Yet now and then, we received random checks that would be for a particular recording that had been made. This recording might possibly encompass concerts we had played in Denmark, Norway, Sweden or anyplace, pieced together. Records were made including tunes which, positively, were only played one time in different concerts which were held in different countries! But they were put together and the money had been paid out but never received by the fellows in the band. Or it was not paid in the correct amounts that should have been paid. I found out later down the line that Basie knew about some of the records being made and he had been paid. But he didn't let on to us even while we were squawking about them.

It didn't really matter that much because it wouldn't have involved more than a few hundred dollars in the pockets of each man. True, at that time a few hundred dollars meant something. Today, it's not that much and only something to laugh about.

Every once in a while on my trips around the world, some fellow would come up to me and say "will you please autograph this album." I'd look at it and ask, "Where did you get this?" He'd answer "I bought it at such and such record shop," maybe in Geneva or Zurich or Rome. The records were out there, all right but I and the other sidemen never received payment for any of them.

We went overseas many times and I'll always remember the time when we were on a tour, going into Paris from some other country. We were supposed to play a theater in Paris that particular night just a few hours after our arrival. Just as soon as we landed, we went to pick up our baggage and instruments. No baggage, no instruments! We waited around, looked for the people in charge of handling our baggage but couldn't find them, either. Finally, about three hours later, someone was finally able to track down where the instruments and baggage were. They

111

were on the way to Caracas, Venezuela!

So there we were in Paris with an engagement to play a theater that night but with no uniforms, no music, no instruments. Naturally, there was nothing we could do but cancel the engagement. We were hoping the baggage would come back from Venezuela the following day and be forwarded to us in Zurich, Switzerland, where we were scheduled to play our next date. We flew on to Zurich, got our hotel rooms and were ready to receive the return of our baggage and instruments. But they did not come in that day, either!

Instead, we were all invited to go to a big party that night and it turned out that we didn't do anything but party in Zurich! One of the young rich entrepreneurs of stocks and bonds was in Zurich at that time. His name was Rosenfeld, I believe. He was a young stock manipulator, had turned over many millions and was in a position to be recognized as a big man among the high flyers of Zurich. He invited all of the band as well as many, many pretty girls. So we just danced and made merry all the rest of the evening. The luggage finally arrived late that night, but by then it was much too late for us to play the engagement, of course.

Zurich was the end of that part of our journey. From that time on, we found other ways of traveling both with and without our instruments, so this wouldn't happen again.

The entire Basie band was booked to play the Royal Festival Hall in London about a month after the opening. This was in 1955 and we were the first jazz orchestra to appear there. We didn't take any music with us because we wanted to travel light and because we were just going over for a short engagement of a week or ten days. This was no problem. The Basie band had been together for some time and every man knew the entire repertoire practically by memory. We left Chicago and flew directly to London, or as directly as you could fly in those days.

We appeared at Royal Festival Hall and when we went on stage, there were only empty chairs, no music stands. We did the complete show, which probably consisted of over two hours of actual playing time and not counting the intermission, and did it all without any music. At first, the audience was aghast that we

112

had no music stands but then they were amazed that we were doing the entire concert without reading any music. It was written up in all of the English papers about how remarkable it was that an orchestra of that size, I think we were seventeen pieces at the time, could play so much and so well without the use of music. We were very highly acclaimed by all the British press.

From London, we went to the continent for the few dates we had around Paris, Brussels and Amsterdam. Then, we were requested to come back to play one final concert at the Royal Festival Hall before we returned to the States. For this appearance, we played an almost entirely different program, again without music! This was a real accomplishment and quite an experience for me to be part of a band that was so professional and so solid that it could be presented and play well under those circumstances. The Basie group was such a tightly-knit group that somehow we were able to carry this off.

I recall a comical incident that happened one time on a flight from London to New York. We were flying in a four-engine Lockheed Constellation. I was sitting in the row behind Basie and everything was going fine. Then, just as we got to the point of no return, I happened to look out the window of the plane and noticed that one of the engines on the port side had a dead propeller which was standing straight up, not moving. The captain hadn't said a word about the fact that we were flying on only three engines.

I tapped Basie on the shoulder and said, "Look out to your left at the inboard motor."

He did and also saw that propeller, which was still standing straight up. I have never seen a fellow express the type of emotion that Count Basie showed then, without saying a single word. He was far from being ecstatic; in fact he was scared as hell. He also knew that we had already passed the point of no return.

Another time, the Basie band was flying to play a job at Fort Bragg, I think it was, in Carolina. We were flying in a U.S. Army plane of the type that was called a "Flying Boxcar," which was strictly for parachutists. We were all on this plane and had parachutes strapped on our back, which was an Army requirement

113

on this type of plane. Before boarding, we each had to sign a waiver that the United States was not at fault in case anything should happen to us while we were in transit.

The seats were placed so that there was a line on each side of the plane, one side facing the other. Count Basie was sitting directly across from me. About fifteen minutes before we got to where we were supposed to land, the pilot decided to check his landing gear to see if everything was in working order. He tried the front landing gear and it was all right. Then he tried the back landing gear. It would not come down.

So there we were up in the air, going into Fort Bragg, fixing to land with no back landing gear! A sergeant came running down the aisle with a broom stick and started gouging at the back landing gear, trying to unlock it. It wouldn't unlock. Then the pilot gave us a message on the loudspeaker. "Due to the back landing gear being stuck, we are going to circle at 5,000 feet. In case we can't get the landing gear down, everyone must prepare to jump."

When he said that, I was looking straight at Count Basie. His eyes were big as saucers. The girl singer, Bixie Crawford, went into hysterics. She was sitting next to me and her tears were flowing like wine. In case we didn't believe this was for real, the sergeant went to the side of the plane, and opened up the door for jumps.

Basie looked at me and asked in a worried voice, "What are we going to do?"

I answered, "I don't know what you're going to do, but as soon as he says 'jump', just give me some room and I'm going to jump out first. I'll let you stay up here if you want to ride around in this plane that can't land."

By that time, Basie's eyes were a little bit larger than saucers and we were still circling at 5,000 feet.

The sergeant went to the back of the plane again with his broom stick. He gouged around for about five minutes and finally the tail landing gear dropped. The pilot told us, "You won't have to jump after all. The landing gear has disengaged itself and we are preparing to land."

That was quite an experience. We finally landed with no

114

trouble at all. The next day, the Army was supposed to fly us on one of these planes from Carolina into Texas, to do a performance there. But when we got on the plane, there were a few guys who had already made their own reservations on the Greyhound bus. They didn't arrive at the job in time and we had to pick up some local musicians to play. It was about four days before we saw these missing fellows again. That was the end of our travels on the Army parachute planes.

On one of our later trips to Europe, we brought along a young lady who sang the blues. This was Vi Redd, the daughter of my old friend, drummer Alton Redd. She had not even been born yet in the early years I worked with Alton. Now, she was a good singer and an equally good alto saxophone player, although at this time, Basie didn't have her play it.

During those years, we were engaged for a few important parties. I remember one we played in the late fifties which was one of the most fantastic parties I have ever seen or even heard of. It was held on a farm in Upperville, Virginia. The owners had designers and builders come to construct the replica of an entire Paris street, complete with buildings, street lights, and so on, *plus* an Indian village with teepees, that was authentic excepting for the running water. This is one of the most amazing things I have ever seen. Among the invited guests were some of the richest people in the world and I recall Jacqueline Kennedy being there. They had a restaurant set up adequate to feed 500 people. When it got very dark one evening, they shot off what we were told was $65,000 worth of fireworks. This was the most tremendous display I have ever seen. At that time, or any other, that was an enormous amount of fireworks. And besides the entire Basie band entertaining, there were four or five other groups, too! This party must have cost millions.

Earlier, I said that I never played again in an organized group with my brother. However, right after Snooky Young left, Basie needed a replacement and Ernie was hired to play the leads on a couple of albums.

It would have been great if we could have continued to work together but there was no way Ernie could think about joining the Basie band. Ernie had been working for about 15 years as a studio musician for ABC, and at the same time, he'd cut one or two recordings in the morning before his regular studio job. He was making a very good living and Basie could not afford to pay him anything like that kind of money. Going on the road with the band would have cut Ernie's gross to probably about one fourth of what he was earning free-lancing and with his contract at ABC. I'd have loved having him in the same band where I was working but the bottom line was making a living.

We always spent quite a lot of time in the Nevada area. While we were there, practically everybody gambled in the casinos. But there was no gambling in the band bus until the latter sixties, when the fellows started playing a dice game called 4-5-6. They would roll three dice in the aisles. We even had a tune called *4-5-6* named after that game! Basie, himself, was an habitual gambler, and he must have gambled away at least a half-million dollars during the time I was with him! He was compulsive and wouldn't leave the game in Vegas until he was busted.

Luckily for Count, he had a very good wife. Catherine Basie never traveled on the road with him. She stayed home and minded their daughter. One day she called him at his New York apartment on Seventh Avenue. She told him it was time for him to come home to his own place. Basie didn't understand what she was talking about but he went to the address she gave him. He was really surprised when he got to this gorgeous home on Long Island because when he walked in, she handed him the keys to this home in St.Albans on Long Island. Then he found out that she had purchased it and it was theirs. For a long time, Catherine had been saving up out of the money he sent home to her every week. It was the first home he ever owned and it remained their home for many years.

Catherine was a fine woman and a marvelous mother. Their only daughter was unfortunately born both physically and mentally handicapped, but she took care of the child in the best way you could imagine. And finally before Basie died, he came to realize what a wonderful wife he had.

During the many years I was with Basie, I enjoyed excellent

116

health excepting now and then I had a little upset stomach. While I was at home for a vacation in the late 1960s, I went to my wife's doctor for a check-up. He was a top man, a physician, surgeon and so on, so I thought I might as well have him look me over. He examined me and said, "There's a very good possibility that you have gallstones. I'd like you to be tested so we'll know for sure."

I said "Okay, let's go ahead with the test."

I only had a few days off at that particular time so he made the appointment for me with a radiologist for the next day. The doctor gave me some pineapple barium to drink, did an examination and found out I really had some big gallstones which needed to be taken out.

As soon as I could, I took off from the band and came home to have the surgery. By this time, Eddie "Lockjaw" Davis had become a force in the Basie band by finagling his way into becoming Basie's road manager. He recommended a fellow in Chicago, who had played at the Club De Lisa with the Red Saunders group, to take my chair. During the time I was out, Lockjaw convinced Basie that he could hire two guys for the price he was paying me and it would help his bankroll. Basie listened and sent me notice that he "was going to have to make a change."

Just like the saying that we had in the band went, "If you get sick, when you are ready to come back, there won't be a job for you," and now it happened to me! This surprised just about everybody in the world except Eddie "Lockjaw" Davis, who hated my guts because he couldn't control me. He had finally grabbed the opportunity, while I was out of commission, to maneuver Basie into getting rid of me so he could have more power. This was the same thing he had done to Charlie Fowlkes. It was Lockjaw who was responsible for getting Charlie fired when he was flat on his back from an accident, even though Charlie was one of oldest members in the new big Basie band. He had it in for anybody he couldn't control and now that included me.

The funny thing is that I was the one who first recommended "Lockjaw" Davis to be in the Basie band! I had heard him playing Monday nights with Bennie Green at Birdland. I arranged for him to meet Basie who then invited him to join the band. And that was how "Lockjaw" showed his appreciation to me!

But it turned out to be a very nice repayment because it was actually the best thing that ever happened to me! I was so enamored of that band that I only thought of going to work and playing, rather than making money. Over the years, I never got any real raises until Tommy Dorsey at one time offered me quite a bit more money than I was getting. When Basie heard about the Tommy Dorsey offer, he immediately raised my salary. I was glad that he did because I wouldn't have been as happy working for Dorsey as Basie.

I left Basie in January of 1970 within a few days of being with the band twenty years. One of the reasons I had stayed with him for so long is that I really didn't have a boss. It's pretty clear that, since I originally went with Count intending to stay only four or five months and ended up being with him twenty years, there must have been a lot of love entwined somewhere for me to remain with him for such a big part of my life. I stuck with this band over the years that we were really scuffling, trying to make it, over the rough periods. And I watched it become a success. Count and I worked together and I can't say that we ever really had an argument over the entire twenty years!

After leaving the Basie band, I immediately got jobs making two and three times my former weekly salary. On top of that, the work was in the Los Angeles area with no hotel bill to pay and no meals to buy outside the home! This move changed the course of my life over the past twenty years and I thank God that I left.

Practically every month afterwards, Basie called begging me to come back. The fellow who had replaced me lasted for about a hot minute and from then on it was musical chairs with one man after the next. I assured Basie that, even though he was my friend and his wife Catherine was a very good friend of my wife, I would never play with him again. We had a very good understanding. He appreciated me, he even gave my wife presents, necklaces and so on. But, as a matter of fact, I never did go back and never did play with him as a bandleader again. And I felt good about the whole thing.

11
The Years After Basie

After leaving Basie, one of my first jobs was playing saxophone at the Ambassador Hotel. The name of the room had just been changed from the Coconut Grove to the Now Grove and I was hired to be in the band organized by George Rhodes, who was Sammy Davis's conductor. To start with, through past friendships and associations, the celebrated trombone player J.J. Johnson had been chosen to be the contractor on the job. But J.J. came out in Los Angeles to get some schooling. He was studying with Earl Hagen, who was then one of the top men for scenario music, compositions for TV and movies. J.J. decided that he didn't want to have a regular job as a trombone player and be the contractor in the band so he asked me if I would take over as contractor. I promptly refused. He said, "Come on Marshal, you can't do this to me. I asked a lot of the guys in the band who they wanted and they all seem to have picked you to replace me."

So I suddenly found out that I was going to be the contractor, which really turned out not to be that bad. The minimum salary I could get was time and a half, which was union scale, plus I was doing three doubles and got extra for that. That is, I was playing clarinet, alto saxophone and flute or piccolo. I wasn't necessarily the best player on those last two but I could play the parts.

I stayed contractor for the George Rhodes band for about ten months or a year. After that, Sammy Davis severed his relationship with the Now Grove. When the next bandleader came in, he asked me if I would remain and be the contractor for the incoming band and shows. I accepted because I didn't have any other job at that time. I conscripted mixed black and white musicians for the Now Grove to be the house band and it was really a very good group.

But this band didn't last because the Now Grove closed down. Luckily, a lot of other things came in for me. I was keeping busy doing recordings again. I began recording when I was just a

119

young whippersnapper, back in the twenties and early thirties. Not many black bands had recording contracts at that time, and those that did had no more than two or three sessions throughout a year. In those days, a session usually meant cutting four sides, which would be issued as both sides of two ten inch records.

One of the very first records I made was with Duke Ellington, in 1934. The tune was *My Old Flame* with Ivie Anderson doing the vocal. I was an added saxophone on that particular session. Around that same time, I played a few other occasions with Duke. With Ellington, it was always a good thing. I appreciated being with him because he was my favorite band leader of all times. That's not putting down any other person that I worked for, but I'm glad I had that experience.

In those early days, I had done little records with groups when I wasn't recognized; people that I have even forgotten about. And, from the time when talking pictures came in, I made many, many recordings for motion pictures. In those days, most of the movies were musicals but the score we played was not necessarily issued on a phonograph record. What we recorded was only for the movie soundtrack. The music sometimes had to be re-recorded due to mechanical problems. As a result the sound track wasn't necessarily played by the band on screen. Part of the music was played by a studio band.

Then, one of my first recordings on which it was actually known that I was involved, was with Art Tatum who was leader of a small group featuring some of the players from the Les Hite band. That was early in 1937. Lloyd Reese was the trumpet player and I was the clarinet. Art, of course, was the piano player and we also had Oscar Bradley on drums and Joe Bailey played bass. We made four sides: *Body and Soul, With Plenty of Money and You, I've Got My Love to Keep Me Warm* and *What Will I Tell My Heart?* While it was a pleasure working with Art Tatum, still in a way it could be very difficult because he played so much piano that there was hardly any room for anybody to play in between the lines.

Later I made quite a few records after Lionel Hampton formed his band. Some of these little things have been forgotten long ago. But then we also did some sessions like the memorable *Flying Home*, which was made with what has become known as "the Flying Home band," the small group within the band.

Aside from making records with a band I was working for, on other sessions I've been specifically hired as a sideman, just to record. Any musician that's received a certain amount of acclaim has had a few experiences in recording studios. I've read about some strange sessions with people who acted in an inappropriate manner but I personally never had any trouble with anybody in the studios. I never worked with any prima donnas, thank God! And I can't remember that Basie ever had any problems with anybody, either. My experiences have all been with professional people who know how to handle themselves and the musicians were controlled by a leader who knew how to lead people. The people who hired me have always expected that I would conduct myself like a gentleman and I have done so. I've liked everybody and most people have liked me.

After World War II, when I was released from the Navy, I recorded almost every week with rock and roll bands. That's the way I made my living for four or five years. During that time, I also made what they call "Race records," which were mostly blues things done for the black southern market. Sometimes, you didn't know where or what you were racing to but they were called Race records. The important thing is, we got paid for making them.

Occasionally, I would get a chance to record with the big studio orchestras with the violins and the harps and everything. This gave me enough beautiful sounds to last me for several months and made up for all the rock and roll I was doing. To put it another way, rock and roll was never my cup of tea, but doing the sessions meant I could buy a whole lot of cups of tea, or whatever I might want to drink.

Along the way, I recorded with many good people. I was with Ray Charles when he did one of his first four-side sessions. At that time, Ray was emulating Nat "King" Cole, both in his singing and playing. I also played on a Dinah Washington session with Gerald Wilson and his band and other local people. For a time after the war, Phil Moore was affiliated with the Discovery

121

Record Company and we did several albums with Lena Horne. I was on many or most of these record sessions made with a 35 piece big band .

I've been hired to do sessions with Frank Sinatra. He's a man who "remembers when." The first time I ever recorded with him was with the Phil Moore Four and One More, in the middle 1940's. We did a session with him before he made the motion picture *From Here To Eternity*, which revitalized his career. To me, the session was symbolic of the times. This man was getting himself together at a time when he was not a big name in the business.

The recording we made is of a tune which probably nobody in this world owns a copy of, a thing called *Bop Goes My Heart*. Can you imagine Frank Sinatra singing "Bop goes my heart?" On top of that, the bass player, Ernie Shepard, did a scat chorus on this song. On Sinatra's record! That's just to show you how times change and how successes can be born and reborn. I was always so happy that Sinatra made it again the way he did, because the man had a lot of heart. And always will have.

Later, during the years I was with Basie, we made sides and albums with just about everybody. We recorded with Tony Bennett, Billy Eckstine, Sarah Vaughan, Frank Sinatra, Ray Charles, Arthur Prysock, and so many, many fine vocalists. It seemed like just about every important singer around wanted to be accompanied by Basie. We were with Judy Garland, doing a command performance for the Queen at the London Palladium, although I am not sure if this was recorded or not.

We even made a record with the Ellington band! Basie and Ellington were recording side by side, the two bandstands in the studio set up with the complete roster of musicians. We tried to pick out tunes that were appropriate to be performed by both bands. This was a little bit discouraging for awhile but during the two separate recording sessions, it was interesting to see how Ellington had arranged and put together little scraps of paper to make an arrangement called *Battle Royal*. It was sort of an exciting tune and a real flag waver, as we call it. Remarkably, it was mixed well enough to make it listenable, so everybody was very happy. This recording is most likely treasured by record collectors.

During the years since I left Basie, that is since 1970, I've been called in to record with just about any big name you can think of. While they are out here in the Los Angeles area, frequently big artists are scheduled to record. If they haven't brought their own musicians and regular set-up with them, they hire local men. I've often been lucky to be one of the people selected.

Sometimes, I have also been asked to help rehearse the group before taping. Going back to my teenage years, I was fortunate in being prepared to take leadership further down in my career. When I attended Jefferson High, I was the concert master in the school orchestra because I was the leading first violin and soloist. The teacher who was in charge of the band and the concert orchestra was a man with a doctorate degree named John Davies. He taught conducting to the concert master, who happened to be me .

During this same time, I was also in the Junior Philharmonic Orchestra. Henry Rockwell, the conductor of the Los Angeles Philharmonic Orchestra, a man of British parentage I believe, also gave me some lessons.

So it happened that I was qualified to help out when the fellows in the Les Hite band asked me to take charge of the band while he was away. Later, I was straw boss for Lionel Hampton and for Count Basie; "assistant" leader of the Navy band. After Basie, I was leader or straw boss for any number of recordings sessions.

Sometimes I am asked what musicians influenced me. When I first started playing clarinet and saxophone, I still thought of myself as a violin player, so what I did on the reeds was just the way I felt like playing. As I was coming up, I heard the music that was being played around Los Angeles and a few jazz records, but not that many bands were making records then. I listened to and admired Louis Armstrong and the Fletcher Henderson Orchestra, and I particularly liked Buster Bailey, Coleman Hawkins, and Earl Hines. On alto saxophone, the men I've admired the most are Johnny Hodges, Benny Carter, and Willie Smith. There have been a lot of other great men over the years but these three stand out for me.

I prefer playing the alto, but my favorite recorded saxophone solo of all time is Coleman Hawkins' recording of *Body and Soul* on tenor. When it was released in 1940, I admired it and I still appreciate what he did because Hawk actually transformed everything about the sound, tone and expression of tenor saxophone. Formerly, fellows played the tenor with a rough edged sound; they honked. But Hawk's delivery was different. From the time that particular record was issued, everyone copied him, forever altering the way tenor sax was played.

Probably my favorite of all saxophone players, who sounded the way I like to hear a saxophone, is Ben Webster. I think that he left behind a tone and a sound that will always be known. He had such a broadness and depth of feeling that it looks to me like no one else can touch him.

I've never been known as a tenor saxophone player. To me, tenor is just another saxophone. When I was young, I just picked it up and played it when it was necessary. There's really not that much difference from one saxophone to the next. It's like you can have ham and eggs or bacon and eggs. I own all the instruments and play them all but I prefer to play alto. However, around 1935 I played tenor when Cab Calloway was appearing for a couple of weeks at the Cotton Club. He was doing a picture, and his tenor sax player, Foots Thomas, was the arranger in his band. Foots had to take off for a week or ten days to write the music that Cab would be playing in the movie so I played tenor with Cab at the same time that Eddie Barefield was the alto and Ben Webster was the other tenor.

After leaving Basie, although I was asked several times, I never did play with a white band so I don't know how I would have liked it. Ernie worked with both the Woody Herman and Stan Kenton bands when he was the only black guy in the band. From what he told me, these experiences were mostly neither embarrassing nor uncomfortable. Later, as I've said, Ernie went to France and stayed there for two or three years while he worked primarily in Jacques Helian's studio orchestra, and while he was over there, he did a few tours too. Of course, the French love jazz and jazz musicians. That's one place where there's not much of a color line.

Ernie and I thought a lot alike but he was more like a son to me than a brother. In appearance, that is to say countenance, we were much alike but he was a head taller than I.

My brother was a wonderful guy, a good listener and he never did anything wrong. He had no enemies in the East in spite of it being really a dog-eat-dog world back there. He was so well thought of in New York that he worked with all the bands around: in theatre bands, Latin bands and what have you. Miles Davis could hardly make a recording with a big band unless he had Ernie as the leader of his trumpet section. Ernie recorded with everyone so that I can turn on the radio and hear record after record made at that time and frequently hear my brother playing.

Ernie was very popular around New York and he was one of the stalwarts at Jim and Andy's bar. Jim was the man who owned the bar and Andy was not his partner; it was his cat. This bar was a popular musician's hangout in Manhattan's upper 50s, a friendly sort of place where all the guys knew each other. Most of the fellows who hung out there were first-line musicians, that is to say, the best there were and they used the place as a call club. Ernie was one of the first "call men" for recordings and for shows in New York. A call man is someone who plays freelance, he is open to all engagements and is usually hired by a phone call: just call and find out if he is available for the date you have in mind. A fellow would give out two phone numbers and if he didn't answer at home, you'd try him at the call club. In case that phone rings, every musician is ready and carries a little appointment book in his pocket or in his instrument case, so he'll know immediately if he is available for the specific date.

In the early seventies, Ernie and I were both hired to do a big extravaganza with Ellington on the West Coast for a show being made for television. Ellington only brought out a nucleus of his band; Harry Carney, Russell Procope, Paul Gonsalves and a few others. The other orchestra members were mostly West Coast musicians hired for the occasion. This was really the only time

Ernie and I were together both playing leads, he on trumpet and me on saxophone. It was a big show and featured Sarah Vaughan, Ray Charles, Peggy Lee, and I believe Joe Williams, too. Ernie and I worked together then for the very last time.

A couple of years ago, I recorded with Linda Ronstadt. This was probably among the last charts which Nelson Riddle arranged and conducted before he died. It was a big band and Linda was just about the sweetest little thing of anybody I've ever met. She was very calm and easy to work with because she had her ears, her heart and her mind open for any suggestions that could be given to help her. I don't know whether the album was truly that successful or not because people usually expected to hear Linda in a different idiom.

Soon after doing that big-band album with her, she hired me as one of the side men to travel with her for an out-of-town engagement of a few weeks. During that particular tour, I was treated about as well as I've ever been treated at any time in my life by anybody. Going to the plane, she had a stretch limousine to pick me up. I was given a number to tie on my baggage. The chauffeur carried my bags and put them on the plane for me and I never saw my luggage again until I got into the hotel. This happened to be the same hotel where Linda was staying. Everything was taken care of. All I had to do was walk to the desk, give my name and they handed me my room key. Before I had been in my room for 30 minutes, her manager called me up to give me a *per diem* for the rest of the week. This was extra money to cover my out of pocket expenses for meals.

On top of all that, Linda put in my pocket as nice a salary as I had ever received from anybody up to that time. And that is one of the best ways of showing appreciation to a musician or anybody you are working with. I have never been better treated for food and all the niceties presented to me. I did then and always will appreciate the most gracious Linda Ronstadt.

Over the years, I have done a lot of traveling. I haven't missed many places in Western Europe. I think my favorite place would be England, because I don't have to worry about having things translated from a different language. About 1980 when I was with the *Ain't Misbehavin'* show for six months in France, I went to a language teacher and studied French. I immediately forget it all when I left France and returned home because I had no one to speak with. I've also visited parts of North Africa such as Tunisia. I've traveled in the East to Japan and been in the Hawaiian Islands. And I've toured South America, most of the big countries there. In my travels, I've had a chance to see racial discrimination in many forms. It is one thing in the United States and another elsewhere.

From my point of view, it sometimes seems that one person is not being prejudiced about another and it's a matter of a person being judged on a racial basis rather than as being an American citizen. Or people will like certain individuals and will stand behind them and press forward to help out a black brother. But that doesn't necessarily mean that 100% of black brothers can do what they would like to do. It's just on an individual basis. That's my way of explaining what happens to black bands and black entertainers.

When I was asked to go to South Africa, a lot of people asked me, "Why do you want to go down there?" They told me that the black man doesn't have a chance, he's in servitude there. I wondered if they were telling the truth or not and decided to see for myself. Before that, a few black athletes like Arthur Ashe had been there and knew what was going on. When I was offered a tour in South Africa, I decided to go and ask for double my usual salary and see how it really was. I thought "I'll grab their money but, before I leave, I'll find out with my own eyes what is happening so I can tell it to friends."

In 1974-75, I was in Johannesberg, Durban, and Soweto, where I played a complete concert for the people of Soweto. Lovelace Watkins, a very talented performer, headed the group. The rest of us, the entertainers and musicians, were always accompanied by the entrepreneur, Wango John. It turned out that we were such a striking success that they wanted us to come back. But we made it clear that we would only come back and play for a mixed audience and provided that the people could sit in any seating that they could buy and pay for. This was agreed upon and

127

it was the first time South Africa had an audience with equal seating for blacks and whites as far as I know.

The best of arrangements were made for us. We stayed at the finest hotels and ate in all the best restaurants. We were treated as "honorary whites". I'm a black man and I became an "honorary white". The others and I would go out and jump in the swimming pool with the rest of the whites, because we wanted to do it. They didn't drain the pool nor did they use it for an inkwell afterwards. We had no trouble whatever. And I was able to come to my own conclusion about exactly what was happening there without someone else telling me about South Africa.

Besides being hired for recordings, over the years I've played a lot of jazz parties and festivals. The largest, earliest and best attended of the festivals in the United States are the Newport Jazz Festival in the New York area and the Monterey Jazz Festival in California. I couldn't say which one was the original festival but the first big one that the Basie band played was at Newport, which was inaugurated by George Wein. The Ellington band also played there and, in fact, it seemed like all of the top musicians in the world who were available were at the Newport Jazz Festival. We played there year after year, and were always well received.

I'll never forget the year at the festival when we were playing in what was supposed to be an enclosed structure. It rained so hard that the bandstand on which we were seated had three or four, maybe five, inches of rain on the floor. It was so deep that it came up over our shoe tops!

During the time that I was with Basie, the Monterey people were hardly hiring any full bands. The jazz groups were mostly smaller, Dixielanders and so on. An eighteen-piece band did not fit in their financial budget during those years. We may have played there a time or two, but that is why the Monterey Jazz Festival was never as important to me, personally, as Newport.

There are other sorts of smaller festival as well. For many years, Dick Gibson and his wife put on a three-day jazz weekend in Colorado every Labor Day. In later years, it was in a Denver hotel. The party was by invitation only, with a limited number of invitees. To my mind, the Gibson weekend was probably the best of this type. I always looked forward to participating because the best musicians available were hired. I especially enjoyed playing with and hearing these men, since many of these were musicians from the East and I am based strictly on the West Coast. That is to say, ordinarily I would not get a chance to see or talk to them.

I played the Gibson party for about ten years. The reason I was chosen is that one day Dick Gibson's wife was listening to an album that I had made on Concord Records. She thought I sounded pretty good, so she suggested to Dick that they should hire me. I played that year and from then on, I was a regular part of their festival every year and we became good friends. The Gibson parties were usually very successful and I've always been proud that they included me in these events.

There is another festival in Minneapolis, which I also enjoy doing annually. The fellows who put this on are stockbrokers or in some such business. They are nice enough always to send a ticket for my wife as well as for me. It makes it convenient for us to be together and have a sort of paid vacation. I appreciate these people very much.

For the past three or four years there has been a concert in San Diego given by a gentleman named Bill Muchnic, a jazz lover and part time trumpet player. There is always a comfortable atmosphere at this festival. Unfortunately, Muchnic died recently but the event still went ahead in 1990. His wife plans to carry on in his fashion, in every respect.

In Europe, there are many, many jazz festivals but I have not played many of them. This is partially because I do not have a European agent. Usually when I go, it is because whoever sends for me pays for my round-trip ticket. Other musicians, 90% of the men who work the festivals, have a European agent. Once you are there, you can be booked in as many countries as you would like to play and can make a complete round of the festivals, going from country to country. But I have never had a regular agent there or anyplace else, for that matter, so anything that comes to me has to come directly from the original person who hired me. Therefore, I have played only a few. Actually, I am not really interested in doing two or three months of continuous engagements in Europe.

The past year was the first time I ever went to England as a single. Susan May, a young English booker, hired me to do a festival in Hayfield. Since I was going to be over there, she used the opportunity to book me into eight or ten other places,too. She was a very good agent for me and really took care of business. As I said, it is no problem getting booked once you are there.

George Wein, who started Newport, also created the Nice Jazz Festival on the French Riviera in the early 1970s. I've appeared there, too, as a single with small groups. Usually this has been in reference to a sort of Basie inspired outfit where the management would use the Basie name as a come-on. Many of us are legitimately ex-Basieites and, to my way of thinking, that certifies us as eligible to call ourselves Basie alumni anywhere in this world. This is not, however, well taken by the Basie administration who don't care for a group taking the Basie name without Basie. But it seems to me that Basie did not make the Basieites; they made Basie!

Recently, that is around the end of 1989, I appeared with a group of ex-Basieites in Japan doing a series of concerts. We were hired by the Japanese as Basie alumni but were forbidden to use the name "Basie" by the current organizers of the Basie band. Even a couple of the members of today's Basie band who were Basieites of 20 years ago were denied the chance to appear in Japan using the Basie name! This happened to John Williams, the baritone sax player who followed Charlie Fowlkes in the band and to Bill Hughes, who was a member of the band from the 50s right up until 1989 and is still there! They could have made quite a bit of money, more than playing with the current Basie band. But they were denied use of the name.

Over the years, I've won a few awards: a life time achievement from a jazz society, best musician of the year some time ago in *Downbeat*, and recognition in various other magazines throughout the years, plus honorable mentions and some small rewards.

When you are playing freelance, you always have to ask

what the uniform is to be. For years and years when I was working in only one place, Sebastian's Cotton Club, on week-ends I always found myself wearing a tuxedo with starched collars and sometimes wing collars. It got to the place where I had a "ring around the collar," I mean a callus around my neck from wearing those starched collars. As an aftermath, even after all these years, I still can not stand to wear tuxedos and anything in that form of dress and won't do it unless I'm forced to by the rules of the group I'm playing with.

One of the nice things that has come out of the latter day, more casual, rules for musicians, is that you can usually select whatever wearing apparel you like, as long as it is reasonably clean. I certainly prefer almost anything to wearing a tuxedo or a uniform.

Starting back in the years when I was in Les Hite's band and all of us had these beautifully made-to-order uniforms, I continued having clothes tailor-made for me. For many years, I never bought a suit off the rack because they didn't fit me right. My shoulders were too broad and my waist too small for an off-the-rack suit.

At one time, everybody had what was known as a "gig suit" which consisted of a matching dark jacket and pants, either very dark blue or black. You'd wear this with a white, soft collar shirt and a tie. However, the last few years, the regular outfit for an average musician has come to be a dark blue coat, grey pants, dark shoes and possibly a red tie, when he is not required to wear a tuxedo.

If I am allowed to wear anything I want for an engagement, my first choice would be clothing that is casual and feels comfortable. When we play, we should not be constricted by our clothing so I like to wear any kind of sport clothing I can feel relaxed in, like turtle necks. But if you leave it to some fellows what to wear, there's no telling how they'll turn up. If you want them to look somewhat decent, you have to have some kind of way of regulating the wearing apparel.

These days, one of the things I like to do most in my leisure time is play golf. I go out even by myself, sign in and play with anyone else who turns up to make a foursome. I also do a whole lot of fishing, which gives a man some time to sit in a boat, do some thinking and enjoy cleansing the mind while fishing. Golf is another story. Sometimes, you need a whole lot of things to cleanse your mind after taking so many bad shots on the golf course. That's the usual thing with me because I've never been a par golfer.

I've always enjoyed outdoor sports since the days Unca Pat took me out and taught me. I used to go hunting in Mexico because it seemed like as soon as it was the first day of shooting, all the birds jumped over the border to the Mexican side and none were left on our side. That meant you had to go hunting below the border. But in recent years, when you get just so far out of the big city, you have to deal with robbers and other people that would take advantage of you. And that includes policemen. They'll nab you for some little infraction like accusing you of having one bird over the limit or something, and then confiscate your good guns. I have a couple of over and under shot guns that sell for $3500 and $4000 each. So mostly I don't go to Mexico anymore. If I have to risk losing my guns, you can bet I only take the cheap ones along.

When I go down to Mexico hunting, I stick with speaking English although I studied Spanish as a high school kid. It was my first class in the morning after working late at night. Sometimes I fell asleep so I didn't learn as much as I could have. On top of that, when I came home and tried to talk with my Mexican friends in the neighborhood, they laughed because I was using Castilian, which was what they taught us in school. The local kids had another dialect and they told me I talked funny.

To keep myself sane, I do a little hunting, play golf, go fishing, and get together once in a while with a few old time friends and other special people. Some of the old friends really are so old that they can't do anything *but* sit down, have a drink and tell a few lies about the old days. I was contemplating going down to Cabo San Lucas on the Baja and doing some marlin fishing because I intend to spend the remaining years of my life doing exactly what I like to do and fishing is one of those.

It's hard to say exactly who my friends were and are. When

you are on the job, you meet many fellows. Sometimes it's just a casual meeting on that particular job. You hang out for awhile and get close. When the job is over, you go one way and the other musicians go the other way. At times you are sorry it's over because you enjoyed yourself so much with one or more particular fellows. And sometimes you are glad the job is over because then you don't have to be with them anymore.

After Evelyn and I were married, our major friendship was with the former band leader, Les Hite and his wife. After his "benefactress" died, he married Lee. Evelyn and I used to spend a lot of our time with Lee and Les and it was always enjoyable. We'd go down to Mexico, to the race track in Agua Caliente, stop at the long bar in Tijuana and things like that. All birthdays and most holidays we'd spend either at the Hites' place or they'd come to ours. Lee and Les were bourbon drinkers and my wife and I were Scotch drinkers. To start off, we'd each have a bottle of what we liked. After all day and all night of listening to records and playing and telling amusing stories, some of it being lies, we would each have consumed our particular bottle of liquor and all of us would be so high that we had to go to sleep on the nearest chair or bed to keep one couple from having to drive home 28 miles through the traffic. That's the type of entertainment we usually had with them.

They had a couple of acres in Monrovia, California. Les had a very easy life with hardly any worries because he had a nice little income and all that property out there. What he liked to do was raise chickens. He had some that were so big you'd think they were turkeys. He had other, Spanish-type chickens and two, three or four imported-type chickens that were just beautiful show poultry.

Les died quite some time ago and as it is now, I don't have too many people to hang out with anymore.

When I was a child, we always went to Sunday services but I no longer go regularly anymore. I believe that everyone should have a religion if it helps them. My wife was raised as a Catholic and went to a convent when she was young but now she is non-denominational. We both believe in God and think that there must have been a stronger force than we are able to see to explain how the world and all came about. It doesn't make us atheists just because we don't belong to any particular religious group.

These days, I'm very comfortable doing exactly what I'm doing. I enjoy playing with good musicians and I only play with people that I like to play with. That's good for me, keeps my head straight. I want to work maybe one or two real good jobs a week and that's enough for me. Over the years, I'll sit down and scribble tunes once in a while. I never did bother about having them published or anything like that. If I can make a record, or play for a TV show or a good casual, that keeps enough money in my pockets to pay the bills and to play the lotteries, too. Who know, maybe one of these days I'll catch a million!

Recording Chronology
by Howard Rye

This discography covers Marshal Royal's jazz and rhythm and blues recordings, so far as information is available, with certain exceptions. He recorded with Count Basie and His Orchestra from 10 April 1951 to 31 December 1969 and again on some sessions in 1973; these recordings are listed in detail in Chris Sheridan, *Count Basie, A Discography*, New York City, Westport, Conn., & London, Greenwood Press, 1986 and also in the relevant volume of Erik Raben's *Jazz Records 1942-1980* (see Bibliography below) and are not repeated here. Marshal Royal has also recorded as a member of the reed section of numerous studio big bands. Among those of possible jazz interest, which might have occasional solos, are recordings with Lorez Alexandria, Cannonball Adderley and His Orchestra, Ray Anthony and His Orchestra, Gordon Jenkins and His Orchestra, Manhattan Transfer, Oliver Nelson's Orchestra, but these are omitted here. There are doubtless many more, especially accompanying popular singers, which have not been identified. However, recordings of this character featuring substantial numbers of personnel drawn from Count Basie's orchestra, but without Basie and not under his name, and therefore not listed in the above sources, have been included as far as possible. No attempt has been made to catalogue unissued concerts, broadcasts and so forth. For reasons of space only original issues are included.

Countries of origin: All records listed are of United States origin unless coded after the label name, as follows:

(E) British; (G) German; (It) Italian

Abbreviations (Instruments, etc.):

a	arranger	as	alto saxophone
b	bass	bar	baritone saxophone
bb	brass bass (tuba or sousa)	bcl	bass-clarinet
bgrd v	background v	bgs	bongos
bj	banjo	btb	bass trombone
c	cornet	cgs	congas
cl	clarinet	cond	conductor
d	drums	dir	director
eb	electric bass	ep	electric piano
f	flute	fh	flugel horn
frh	french horn	h	harmonica
g	guitar	kbrds	keyboards
ldr	leader	p	piano
o	organ	ob	oboe
perc	percussion	pic	piccolo
sb	double bass	ss	soprano saxophone
t	trumpet	tb	trombone
ts	tenor saxophone	v	vocal
vb	vibraphone	vc	violoncello
v n	violin	vtb	valve-trombone

Abbreviations (Other):

CD	Compact Disc
LP	Long-Playing Record

Recording Chronology

Acknowledgements: For assistance in compiling this discography thanks are due to Les Fancourt, Alyn Shipton, Peter Vacher, Bob Weir, and the staff of the British Library National Sound Archive and British Film Institute Library.

Bibliography:
The following works have been consulted:
Erik M. Bakker & Coen Hoffmann, 'Crown Research' in *Names & Numbers 1* (April 1985).
Anthony Barnett, 'Ray Perry: The Rosencrantz Transcriptions And Other Violin Recordings', *Fable Bulletin: Violin Improvisation Studies*, No. 2, Lewis, East Sussex, 1993.
Walter Bruynincx, *70 Years Of Recorded Jazz: 1917-1987*, Mechelen, Belgium, 1987- (in progress).
Walter Bruynincx, *Modern Discography, Modern Jazz: Be-Bop, Hard Bop, West Coast* (6 vols), Mechelen, Belgium, 1984-1987.
Walter Bruynincx, *Swing Discography, Swing//1920-1985, Swing/Dance Bands & Combos* (12 vols), Mechelen, Belgium, 1986-1990.
Walter Bruynincx, *Traditional Discography, Traditional Jazz//1897-1985, Origins/New Orleans/Dixieland/Chicago Styles* (6 vols), Mechelen, Belgium, 1987-1990.
Walter Bruynincx, *Vocalists Discography, The Vocalists 1917-1986, Singers & Crooners*, Mechelen, Belgium, 1989-1990.
Buck Clayton with Nancy Miller Elliott, *Buck Clayton's Jazz World*, London, 1986.
Richard Cook & Brian Morton, *The Penguin Guide To Jazz On CD, LP & Cassette*, London, 1994.
Mike Doyle & Peter Lowe, 'Slim Gaillard Discography', *Discographical Forum*, 49/50 (1985).
Charles Garrod, *Four Star And Gilt Edge Records*, Zephyrhills, Fla., 1993.
John Kisch & Edward Mapp, *A Separate Cinema*, New York City, 1992.
Arnold Laubich & Ray Spencer, *Art Tatum, A Guide To His Recorded Music*, Metuchen, N.J. & London, 1982.
Mike Leadbitter & Neil Slaven, *Blues Records 1943-1970, A Selective Discography, Volume One A To K*, London, 1987.
Mike Leadbitter, Leslie Fancourt & Paul Pelletier, *Blues Records 1943-1970, "The Bible Of The Blues"*, Volume Two L To Z, London, 1994.
Jay Robert Nash & Stanley Ralph Ross, *The Motion Picture Guide, 1927-1983*, Chicago, 1986.
Vincent Pelote, 'Discography' in Lionel Hampton with James Haskins, *Hamp, An Autobiography*, New York City, 1989.
Jordi Pujol, insert notes for 'Ray Charles: The Birth Of A Legend', Ebony CD8001/8002, 1992.

Erik Raben (ed.), *Jazz Records 1942-80, A Discography*, Copenhagen, 1989- (in progress).

Michel Ruppli, *The Aladdin/Imperial Labels, A Discography*, Westport, CT, & London, 1991.

Michel Ruppli, *Atlantic Records, A Discography, Volume 1*, Westport, CT, & London, 1979.

Michel Ruppli, *The Clef/Verve Labels, A Discography*, Westport, CT, & London, 1986.

Michel Ruppli, *The King Labels, A Discography*, Westport, CT, & London, 1985.

Michel Ruppli, *The Savoy Label, A Discography*, Westport, CT, & London, 1980.

Michel Ruppli & Ed Novitsky, *The Mercury Labels, A Discography*, Westport, CT, & London, 1993.

Brian Rust, *Jazz Records 1897-1942*, 5th Revised and Enlarged Edition, Chigwell, Essex, England, n.d [1984].

Roy Simonds, *King Curtis, A Discography*, Edgware, Middlesex, 1984.

Dr. Klaus Stratemann, *Negro Bands On Film, Volume 1, Big Bands 1928-1950, An Exploratory Filmo-Discography*, Lübbecke, Germany, 1981.

Dr. Klaus Stratemann, *Duke Ellington Day By Day And Film By Film*, Copenhagen, 1992.

Various editions of the *Bielefelder Katalog Jazz* (ed. Manfred Scheffner), and of the following magazines: *Bulletin du Hcf, Collectors Items, Jerry's Rhythm Rag, Monthly Film Bulletin, Storyville.*

LES HITE AND HIS ORCHESTRA On Film

Les Hite And His Orchestra took part in a number of film soundtracks recorded in Hollywood, Cal. in the 1930s, some of which have yet to be identified by researchers. Furthermore, as Marshal Royal himself points out, the band's presence on screen does not necessarily mean that they are to be heard on the soundtrack. Where they are heard, they may be augmented by studio musicians, adding to the difficulty of making reliable aural identifications under typical viewing conditions and possibly with overdubbed dialogue. The following listing of films in which the band is thought to be heard is therefore both tentative and incomplete. As far as is known, none has yet appeared on a commercial record, except as noted.

TAXI (Warner Brothers) dir. Roy Del Ruth   1931

      China Boy
      Darktown Strutters' Ball
      Georgia On My Mind
      I Need Lovin'
      Dinah

CABIN IN THE COTTON (Warner Brothers) dir. Michael Curtiz   1933

      Willie The Weeper
      Peckerwoods Wiggle
      Willie The Weeper (Bette Davis, v)

I'M NO ANGEL (Paramount Pictures) dir. Wesley Ruggles   1933
      Sister Honky Tonk (Mae West, v)
      I'm Just Wild About My Dallas Man (Mae West, v)
      I'm No Angel (Mae West, v)

CAVALCADE (Fox Film Corporation) dir. Frank Lloyd   1933
      Twentieth Century Blues (Una O'Connor, v)

SING, SINNER, SING (Majestic Pictures) dir. Howard Christy   1933
The Motion Picture Guide states that this film is "packed with jazz and cabaret stock footage."

THE MUSIC GOES ROUND (Columbia Pictures) dir. Victor Schertzinger 1936
      Life Begins When You're In Love
      Susannah, I'm Betting On You

BARGAIN WITH BULLETS (Million Dollar Productions) dir. Ralph Cooper
                                                   1937

The band is credited as **Les Hite's Cotton Club Orchestra**.

This film was also released as *Gangsters On The Loose*, which some sources claim is the original title.

MURDER IN SWINGTIME (Condor Pictures) dir. Arthur Dreifuss   1937
>Dinah
>
>What's Music Got (That I Ain't Got) (June Richmond, v)
>
>Dinah (Peppy Prince, v)

FOOLS FOR SCANDAL (Warner Brothers) dir. Mervyn LeRoy   1938
>Just A Simple Melody
>
>There's A Boy In Harlem (Jeni Le Gon, The Three Brown Sisters, v)

AT THE CIRCUS (Metro-Goldwyn-Meyer) dir. Edward Buzzell   1939
>Swingali (unknown male, v; unknown female, 2nd v; child vocal chorus)
>
>Blue Moon (Harpo Marx, harp)
>
>Swing Low, Sweet Chariot (Harpo Marx, harp; mixed v chorus)

There have been commercial video releases of this film.

EARL DANCER AND HIS ORCHESTRA
Unidentified group, inc. Buck Clayton, t; Parker Berry, tb; Marshal Royal, cl; Preston
'Peppy' Prince, d; Earl Dancer, dir; Glenda Farrell, v-1.

Hollywood, Cal.		1933
I Want A Man -1		unissued
unidentified title		unissued

These titles are from the soundtrack of the Columbia Pictures film *Lady For A Day*, dir.
Frank Capra. According to Buck Clayton, Earl Dancer recruited bands for film work only,
using musicians from several Los Angeles based bands including Les Hite's, and they may
well appear in other films not yet identified.

DUKE ELLINGTON AND HIS ORCHESTRA
Arthur Whetsel, Freddie Jenkins, Cootie Williams, t; Joe Nanton, Lawrence Brown, tb; Juan
Tizol, vtb; Barney Bigard, cl/ts; Johnny Hodges, ss/as, Marshal Royal or Otto Hardwick,
as; Harry Carney, bar/bcl; Duke Ellington, p; Fred Guy, g; Wellman Braud, sb; Sonny Greer,
d; Barbara Van Brunt, v (overdubbed).

Hollywood, Cal.	26 February 1934
Ebony Rhapsody	unissued

The above title was recorded for the soundtrack of the Paramount film *Murder At The
Vanities.*, dir. Mitchell Leisen. The vocal by Barbara Van Brunt was overdubbed on 16
April 1934. Marshal Royal himself states that he performed in the version used in the film
but all other sources give Hardwick. Marshal Royal may well be present on a rejected
version recorded on 18 March 1934 with vocal by Gertrude Michael, who in the event
appeared on screen voiced by Barbara Van Brunt. The dating of Marshal Royal's period
substitituting for Otto Hardwick is considered in detail by Stratemann, *Duke Ellington*,
p.87.

Arthur Whetsel, Freddie Jenkins, Cootie Williams, t; Joe Nanton, Lawrence Brown, tb; Juan
Tizol, vtb; Barney Bigard, cl/ts; Johnny Hodges, Marshal Royal (or Otto Hardwick-1), as;
Harry Carney, bar; Duke Ellington, p; Fred Guy, g; Wellman Braud, sb/bb; Sonny Greer, d;
Mae West, v.

Hollywood, Cal.	15 March 1934
When A St. Louis Woman -1	*FDC(It) 1021 [LP]*
Hollywood, Cal.	16 March 1934
Memphis Blues -1	*Extreme Rarities* *ER1004 [LP]*
Hollywood, Cal.	24 March 1934
79181-A My Old Flame	*RCA 9971-2-R* *[CD]*
Hollywood, Cal.	26 March 1934

Hesitation Blues   *FDC(It) 1021 [LP]*

The above titles were recorded for the soundtrack of the Paramount film *Belle Of The Nineties*, dir. Leo McCarey. The LPs are dubbed from the soundtrack, and are edited versions of the original pre-recordings. The third title was transcribed in April 1934 onto a Victor master which is issued complete on the CD indicated. A slightly edited version was originally issued on Biltmore 1014. It is not certain that Marshal Royal is present on the 15 & 16 March dates, which may feature Otto Hardwick, as. Other titles used in the film and issued on various records are from sessions in May 1934 in which Marshal Royal did not take part.

LARRY ADLER with DUKE ELLINGTON AND HIS ORCHESTRA
Unknown, t; unknown, tb; Barney Bigard, cl/ts; Johnny Hodges, Marshal Royal, as; Harry Carney, bar; Duke Ellington, p; Fred Guy, g; Wellman Braud, sb; Sonny Greer, d; Larry Adler, h.

Hollywood, Cal.		21 March 1934
	Sophisticated Lady	*Up-To-Date 2009*
		(LP)

The above title was recorded for the soundtrack of the Paramount film *Many Happy Returns*, dir. Norman Z. McLeod. Ten musicians were used and the unknowns are drawn from the Ellington trumpet and trombone sections (see previous entry). It is not certain that Marshal Royal, rather than Otto Hardwick, appears on this recording.

DUKE ELLINGTON AND HIS ORCHESTRA
Arthur Whetsel, Cootie Williams, t; Joe Nanton, Lawrence Brown, tb; Juan Tizol, vtb; Barney Bigard, cl/ts; Johnny Hodges, cl/as/ss; Harry Carney, cl/as/bar; Marshal Royal, cl/as; Duke Ellington, p; Fred Guy, g; Wellman Braud, sb; Sonny Greer, d; Ivie Anderson, v.

Hollywood, Cal.		9 May 1934
79211-2	Troubled Waters	Victor 24651
79212-2	My Old Flame	Victor 24651

LES HITE AND HIS ORCHESTRA
George Orendorff, James Porter, Harold Scott, t; Parker Berry, Sonny Craven, tb; Les Hite, Marshal Royal, Marvin Johnson, as; Charlie Jones, ts; Henry Prince, Harvey Brooks, p; Bill Perkins, g; Joe Bailey, sb; Preston 'Peppy' Prince, d/v-1.

Los Angeles, Cal.		6 June 1935
LA-373-	Chant Of Mustard Green	ARC unissued
LA-374-	It Must Have Been A Dream -1	ARC unissued
Los Angeles, Cal.		15 August 1935
LA-1070-	No-One Is To Blame	ARC unissued
LA-1071-	Young Stuff	ARC unissued

[MGM studio orchestra]
Unknown instrumentation and personnel, including Mannie Klein, t; poss. Marshal Royal,

as; Harpo Marx, f; Ivie Anderson, v-1; The Crinoline Choir, v; Leo Arnaud, a.

Hollywood, Cal.   late 1936 or early
                                                                         1937

    Who's Dat Man (It's Gabriel)   *Black Jack(G)*
                                                                         3004 [LP]

    All God's Chillun Got Rhythm -1   *Black Jack(G)*
                                                                         3004 [LP]

The above titles are from the soundtrack of the MGM film *A Day At The Races*, dir. Sam Wood. Marshal Royal himself considers that he took part in it as a member of the studio orchestra. It does not appear to involve other Les Hite personnel. The LP is incorrectly credited to **Duke Ellington And His Famous Orchestra**.

ART TATUM AND HIS SWINGSTERS
Lloyd Reese, t; Marshal Royal, cl; Art Tatum, p/cel-1; Bill Perkins, g; Joe Bailey, sb; Oscar Bradley, d.

    Los Angeles, Cal.   26 February 1937
DLA-724-A Body And Soul   Decca 1197
DLA-724-B Body And Soul   *MCA(F) 510.123*
                                                                         (LP)
DLA-725-A With Plenty Of Money And You   Decca 1198
DLA-725-B With Plenty Of Money And You   *MCA(F) 510.123*
                                                                         (LP)
DLA-726-A What Will I Tell My Heart -1   Decca 1197
DLA-727-A I've Got My Love To Keep Me Wram   Decca 1198

Marshal Royal has been named in some sources as a member of the orchestra which accompanied Louis Armstrong in the 1937 Paramount film *Every Day's A Holiday*, dir. A. Edward Sutherland, but other sources indicate that the accompaniment is by Eddie Barefield's Orchestra without Marshal.

LIONEL HAMPTON AND HIS SEXTETTE
Marshal Royal, cl-1/as-2; Ray Perry, as-3/vn-4; Sir Charles Thompson, p; Irving Ashby, g; Vernon Alley, sb; Lee Young, d/v-5; Lionel Hampton, vb; Evelyn Myers, v-6; The Rhythm Girls, v-5.

    Hollywood, Cal.   19 December 1940
055228-1   Lost Love -2, 3, 5   Victor 27278
055229-1   I Nearly Lost My Mind -1, 3, 6   Victor 27316
055230-1   Altitude -1, 3, 4   Victor 27316
055231-1   Fiddle-Dee-Dee -1, 4   Victor 27364

Marshal Royal, cl-1/as-2; Ray Perry, as-3/vn-4; Sir Charles Thompson, p-5; Irving Ashby, g; Vernon Alley, sb; Lee Young, d; Lionel Hampton, vb-6/p-7/v-8; The Rhythm Girls, v-8.

    Hollywood, Cal.   20 December 1940
055234-1   Bogo Joe -1, 4, 5, 6, 8   Victor 27341

055235-1	Open House -1, 3, 4, 5, 6	Victor 27341
055236-1	Smart Alec -1, 3, 4, 5, 6	Victor 27278
055237-1	Bouncing At The Beacon -2, 7	Victor 27364

Though all existing sources give Hampton as the only pianist on matrix 055237-1, it seems aurally likely that he plays only the treble part and that the bass part is played by Sir Charles Thompson.

Karl George, t; Marshal Royal, cl; Ray Perry, as-1/vn-2; Sir Charles Thompson, p; Irving Ashby, g; Vernon Alley, sb; Shadow Wilson, d-3; Lionel Hampton, vb-4/d-5/v-6; Rubel Blakey, v-7; ensemble v-6.

Hollywood, Cal.		8 April 1941
064005-2	Give Me Some Skin -1, 2, 3, 4, 6, 7	Victor 27409
064056-1	Now That You're Mine -1, 3, 4, 7	Victor 27529
064057-1	Chasin' With Chase -1, 5	Victor 27529
064058-1	Three-Quarter Boogie -2, 3, 4	Victor 27409

LIONEL HAMPTON AND HIS ORCHESTRA

Karl George, Ernie Royal, Joe Newman, t; Fred Beckett, Sonny Craven, Harry Sloan, tb; Marshal Royal, cl/as; Ray Perry, as; Dexter Gordon, Illinois Jacquet, ts; Jack McVea, bar; Milton Buckner, p; Irving Ashby, g; Vernon Alley, sb; George Jenkins, d; Lionel Hampton, vb-1/v-2; Rubel Blakey, v-3.

New York City.		24 December 1941
70100-A	Just For You -1, 3	Decca 18265
70101-A	Southern Echoes -2	Decca 18285
70102-A	My Wish -1, 3	Decca 18265
70103-A	Nola -1	Decca 18285

LIONEL HAMPTON SEXTET

Marshal Royal, cl; Jack McVea, bar; Ray Perry, vn-1; Milton Buckner, p; Irving Ashby, g; Vernon Alley, sb; George Jenkins, d; Lionel Hampton, vb/v-2.

New York City.		2 March 1942
70416-A	Royal Family -1	*Brunswick(G)*
		87526LPBM (LP)
70417-A	I Can't Believe That You're In Love With Me	*Brunswick(G)*
		87526LPBM (LP)
70418-A	Blues In The News -1	*Brunswick(G)*
		87526LPBM (LP)
70419-A	Exactly Like You -1, 2	*Brunswick(G)*
		87526LPBM (LP)

Most sources give Ray Perry as the baritone saxophonist as well as the violinist, but it is impossible for this to be correct.

LIONEL HAMPTON AND HIS ORCHESTRA
Ernie Royal, Karl George, Jack Trainer, Eddie Hutchinson or Manny Klein, t; Fred Beckett,
Sonny Craven, Harry Sloan, tb; Marshal Royal, cl/as; Ray Perry, as; Bob Barefield,
Illinois Jacquet, ts; Jack McVea, bar; Milton Buckner, p; Irving Ashby, g; Vernon Alley, sb;
Lee Young, d; Lionel Hampton, vb/a-1; Rubel Blakey, v-2; Clyde Hart, a-3.

	New York City.	26 May 1942
70771-A	Now I Know -2	Decca 18535
70772-A	Half A Loaf Is Better Than None -2	Decca 18535
70773-A	Flying Home -1	Decca 18535
70774-A	In The Bag -3	Decca 18535

The personnel for this session has been the subject of much controversy. That quoted is taken
from the fifth edition of *Jazz Records 1897-1942*, with the addition of Karl George, whom
all other sources believe to be the trumpet soloist heard on *In The Bag*. All sources agree on
the presence of the trombonists named, both Royal brothers, Perry, Jacquet, McVea, and
Buckner, but alternative proposals have been made for all other chairs. As only four
trumpeters are present, one of those listed in *Jazz Records* must be absent if George is
present. The naming of Klein, a white studio musician, may seem particularly contentious
but by the same token he is unlikely to have been proposed without evidence.

Marshal Royal is listed in some sources for Black and White matrices BW-114 to BW-117
by Jack McVea & His All Stars (c.October 1945), but McVea is the only reed player heard.

BOB MOSLEY AND HIS ALL STARS
Karl George, t; Marshal Royal, cl-1/as-2; Lucky Thompson, ts; Bob Mosley, p; Gene
Phillips, g; Charlie Mingus, sb; Lee Young, d; Marion Abernathy, v-3.

	Los Angeles, Cal.	c. November 1945
BTJ-34-3	Voot Rhythm -2	BelTone 751
BTJ-35-1	Stormy Mood -1, 2, 3	BelTone 752
BTJ-36-2/3	Baggin' The Boogie -1, 2, 3	BelTone 751
BTJ-37-5	Bee Boogie Boo -1	BelTone 752

DUKE HENDERSON & JACK McVEA ALL STARS
Prob. Jesse Perdue, t; Marshal Royal, as; Jack McVea, ts; Bob Mosley, p; Frank Clarke, sb;
Rabon Tarrant, d; Duke Henderson, v.

	Los Angeles, Cal.	5 December 1945
S-1163	Oo Wee Baby, Oo Wee	Apollo 367
S-1664	Fool Hearted Woman	Apollo 373
S-1165	Lottery Blues	Apollo 373
S-1166	Wiggle Wiggle Woogie	Apollo 367

RABON TARRANT with JACK McVEA & HIS BAND
Prob. Jesse Perdue, t; Marshal Royal, as; Jack McVea, ts; John Shackleford, p; Frank Clarke,
sb; Rabon Tarrant, d/v-1.

	Los Angeles, Cal.	December 1945

Recording Chronology

S-1167	Blues This Morning -1	Apollo 377
S-1169	Opus Boogie	Apollo 377

Matrix S-1168 is untraced.

EDDIE HEYWOOD SEXTET

Henry 'Parr' Jones, t; Vic Dickenson, Henry Coker, tb; Marshal Royal, as; Eddie Heywood, p; Ernest Shepard, sb; Charlie Blackwell, d.

	Los Angeles, Cal.	3 December 1945
L-4010-	On The Sunny Side Of The Street	Decca 23534
L-4011-	The Man I Love	Decca 23534

JACK McVEA & HIS ALL STARS

Jesse Perdue, t; Marshal Royal, cl/as; Jack McVea, ts/a-1; John Shackleford, p; Frank Clarke, sb; Rabon Tarrant, d; Estelle Edson, v-2.

	Los Angeles, Cal.	January 1946
BW-167	Play It Over -1	Black & White 762
BW-168	House Party Boogie	Black & White 762
BW-169-1	My Business Is C.O.D. -2	Black & White 763
BW-170-2	Baby Make Up Your Mind -2	Black & White 763

SLIM GAILLARD AND HIS ORCHESTRA

Howard McGhee, t; Marshal Royal, cl; Lucky Thompson, ts; Dodo Marmarosa, p; Slim Gaillard, g/v-1; Bam Brown, sb/v-2; Zutty Singleton, d.

	Los Angeles, Cal.	January 1946
BTJ-58-3	Chicken Rhythm -1, 2	BelTone 762
BTJ-59-1	Santa Monica Jump	BelTone 761
BTJ-60-1	Mean Pretty Mama -1	BelTone 762
BTJ-61-2	School Kids' Hop -1, 2	BelTone 758

EDDIE HEYWOOD SEXTET

Henry 'Parr' Jones, t; Vic Dickenson, Henry Coker, tb; Marshal Royal, as; Eddie Heywood, p; Ernest Shepard, sb; William 'Keg' Purnell, d.

	New York City.	7 February 1946
73351-	On The Alamo	Decca 23811
73352-	I Didn't Know About You	*Decca DL8270 (LP)*
73353-	Just You, Just Me	*Decca DL8270 (LP)*

Henry 'Parr' Jones, t; Britt Woodman, Henry Coker, tb; Marshal Royal, as; Eddie Heywood, p; Ernest Shepard, sb; William 'Keg' Purnell, d.

New York City.		29 February 1946
73486-	Sweet And Lovely	Decca 23813
73487-	Who's Sorry Now	Decca 23813
73488-	Loch Lomond	Decca 23590
73489-	Pom Pom	Decca 24604

EDDIE HEYWOOD AND HIS ORCHESTRA

Henry 'Parr' Jones, t; Britt Woodman, Henry Coker, tb; Marshal Royal, as; Eddie Heywood, p; Ernest Shepard, sb; William 'Keg' Purnell, d.

New York City.		5 April 1946
73494-	I Don't Know Why	Decca unissued
73495-	Temptation	Decca 23811
73496-	Heywood's Blues	Decca 23677

BARON MINGUS AND HIS OCTET

Karl George, t; Henry Coker, tb; Marshal Royal, cl/as; Willie Smith, as; Lucky Thompson, ts; Lady Will Carr, p; Irving Ashby, g; Charles Mingus, sb; Lee Young, d; Claude Trenier, v-1.

Los Angeles, Cal.		11 April 1946
382-AS-	Ashby De La Zooch	4 Star 1105
383-AS-	Love On A Greyhound Bus	4 Star 1105

This record was probably never released.

Los Angeles, Cal.		20 April 1946
393-AS-	Bedspread	4 Star 1107
394-AS-1	Honey Take A Chance With Me -1	4 Star 1108
395-AS-	Make Believe	4 Star 1107
396-AS-2	This Subdues My Passion	4 Star 1108
397-AS-	Pipe Dreams	4 Star 1106
398-AS-	After Hours	4 Star 1106

JACK McVEA AND HIS DOOR OPENERS

Joe Kelly, t; Melba Liston, tb; Marshal Royal, cl/as; Jack McVea, ts; Tommy 'Crow' Kahn, p; Irving Ashby, g; Frank Clarke, sb; Rabon Tarrant, d/v.

Los Angeles, Cal.		c. October 1946
BW-433	Basses Boogie	Black & White 808
BW-434	Boilermaker's Boogie	Black & White 808
BW-435	Blackout Boogie	Black & White 809
BW-436	Hangover Boogie	Black & White 811

147

BW-437	Baby It's Fun	Black & White 811
BW-438	Reetie Vootie Boogie	Black & White 809
BW-439	Groovin' Boogie	Black & White 810
BW-440	Barrelhouse Boogie	Black & White 810

LENA HORNE with PHIL MOORE ORCHESTRA

Gerald Wilson, t; Murray McEachern, tb; Willie Smith, cl/as; Marshal Royal, cl/ts; Phil Moore, p; Irving Ashby, g; Red Callender, sb; Lee Young, d; Lena Horne, v.

Los Angeles, Cal. — Fall 1946

BW-516	Whispering	Black & White 815
BW-518	Squeeze Me	Black & White 819
BW-519	You Go To My Head	Black & White 819

It is probable that Marshal Royal is present on other Black & White recordings by Lena Horne with the Phil Moore Orchestra, but these have not been reliably identified.

PHIL MOORE ORCHESTRA

Snooky Young, Ray Linn, Gerald Wilson, t; Henry Coker, Murray McEachern, Ben Benson, tb; Harry Schumann, frh; Harry Klee, f; Marshal Royal, cl/as; Lucky Thompson, ts; unknowns, strings; Calvin Jackson, p; Al Hendrickson, g; Red Callender or Art Shapiro, sb; Lee Young, d; Phil Moore, dir.

Los Angeles, Cal. — 1947

D-101	Concerto For Piano And Orchestra, Pt. 1	Discovery 1200
D-102	Concerto For Piano And Orchestra, Pt. 2	Discovery 1200
D-103	Concerto For Piano And Orchestra, Pt. 3	Discovery 1200
D-104	Concerto For Piano And Orchestra, Pt. 4	Discovery 1200
D-105	Concerto For Trombone, Pt. 1	Discovery 1200
D-106	Concerto For Trombone, Pt. 2	Discovery 1200
D-107	Fugue For Bar Room Piano	Discovery 101
D-108	Misty Moon Blues	Discovery 101
D-109	Day Dream	*Verve MGV2005 (LP)*
D-110	125th Street Prophet	Discovery 100
D-111	Cornucopia	Discovery 100
D-112	I Can't Get Started	Discovery 112
D-113	Lover	Discovery 111
D-114	Prelude In C-Sharp Minor	Discovery 112

D-115	Blue Skies	Discovery 110
D-116	Laura	Discovery 110
D-117	Gershwin Prelude	Discovery unissued
D-118	Blues In The Night	Discovery unissued
D-119	Lady Be Good	Discovery 111
	Fantasy For Girl And Orchestra	*Verve MGV2005 (LP)*
	Mood For You	*Verve MGV2005 (LP)*

According to some sources, Discovery 110, 111, 112 are credited to **Calvin Jackson**. Discovery 1200 is a 78 r.p.m. album.

Los Angeles, Cal.		1947
D-130	Fantasy For Strings, Pt. 1	*Discovery DL4002 (LP)*
D-131	Fantasy For Strings, Pt. 2	*Discovery DL4002 (LP)*
D-132	Fantasy For Strings, Pt. 3	*Discovery DL4002 (LP)*

PERCY MAYFIELD with MONROE TUCKER & HIS ORCHESTRA
Vernon Smith, t; Marshal Royal, as; Maxwell Davis, ts; Floyd Turnham, bar; Willard McDaniel, p; Chuck Norris, g; Roy Hamilton, sb; Henry Williams, d; Percy Mayfield, v.

Los Angeles, Cal.		1947
Su-227	Half Awake (Baby You're Still A Square)	Supreme 1543
Su-228	Two Years Of Torture	Supreme 1543
Su-229	How Wrong Can A Good Man Be	Supreme 1549
Su-230	Leary Blues	Supreme 1549

GENE PHILLIPS & HIS RHYTHM ACES
Jake Porter, t; Marshal Royal, as; Maxwell Davis, ts; Lloyd Glenn, p; Gene Phillips, g/v; Arthur Edwards, sb; William Streets, d; band v-1; band members, sp-2.

Los Angeles, Cal.		1947
MM-301-3	Stinkin' Drunk	Modern 20-586
MM-302-2	I Could Make You Love Me	Modern 148
MM-303-4	Boogie Everywhere	Modern 148
	Short Haired Ugly Woman	*Ace(E) CHD169 (LP)*

Evidence for assigning the fourth, originally unissued, title to this session is not known.

| Los Angeles, Cal. | | 1947 |
| MM-532-4 | Big Fat Mama | Modern 20-519 |

MM-533-3	Three O'Clock In The Morning	Modern 20-519

	Los Angeles, Cal.	1947
MM-589-3	Big Legs	Modern 20-527
MM-590-4	Hey Lawdy Mama -1	Modern 20-572
MM-591-4	It Was Just A Dream	Modern 20-527
MM-592-3	Honey Chile -2	Modern 20-625

	Los Angeles, Cal.	1947
MM-636-2	Punkin' Head Woman	Modern 20-559
MM-637-3	Fatso	Modern 20-546
MM-639-4	Rock Bottom -1	Modern 20-546

Matrix MM-638 is untraced.

It is possible that Marshal Royal is present on subsequent recordings by Gene Phillips.

GERALD WILSON ORCHESTRA

Big band including: Gerald Wilson, t; Melba Liston, tb; Marshal Royal, cl/as; Floyd Turnham, Maurice Simon, ts; Jimmy Bunn, p; Charles E. Thompson, d; Robert Budd, Elijah Harper, unknown instruments.

	Los Angeles, Cal.	13 March 1947
129	The Prince Strikes Back	Aladdin 534
131	Whistler's Blues	Aladdin 534
	Washboard Blues	Aladdin 535
	Undercover Blues	Aladdin 535

LLOYD GLENN AND HIS JOYMAKERS

Jake Porter, t; Marshal Royal, as; Gene Porter, ts; Lloyd Glenn, p; Gene Phillips, g; Arthur Edwards, sb; William Streets, d; Geraldine 'Jerry' Carter, v-1

	Los Angeles, Cal.	December 1947
IM-41	Joymaker's Boogie	Imperial 5031
IM-42	Advice To A Fool -1	Imperial 5031
IM-43	That Other Woman's Got To Go -1	Imperial 5022
IM-44	Rampart St. Jump	Imperial 5022

Contrary to some previous discographies, Marshal Royal is to be heard on all titles from this session and is not present at all on matrices IM-67 to IM-71 from the session on 26 December 1947.

FRANK SINATRA with PHIL MOORE FOUR

Marshal Royal, as; Phil Moore, p; unknown, g; Ernie Shepard, sb; unknown, d; Frank Sinatra, v.

	Los Angeles, Cal.	15 December 1948
HCO-3475	Why Can't You Behave	Columbia 38393
HCO-3476	Bop! Goes My Heart	Columbia 38421

Marshal Royal recalled his own presence on this session, which is listed in existing sources as accompanied by piano and rhythm only.

MARY ANN McCALL with PHIL MOORE ORCHESTRA

Gerald Wilson, t; Murray McEachern, tb; Marshal Royal, as/cl; Harry Klee, ts/f; Harry Schumann, ts/bar; Tommy Todd, p; Jack Marshal, g; Ernie Shepard, sb; Lee Young, d.

	Los Angeles, Cal.	27 December 1948
D-133	You're My Thrill	Discovery 509
D-134	I Hadn't Anyone Till You	Discovery 502
D-135	You're Mine You	Discovery 502

	Los Angeles, Cal.	3 January 1949
D-136-4	I'm Yours	Discovery 512
D-137-4	Nice Work If You Can Get It	Discovery 512
D-138	Sunday	Discovery 509

MARION ABERNATHY

Joe Newman, t; Henry Coker, tb; Marshal Royal, cl/as; Bumps Myers, ts; Maurice Simon, bar; Gerald Wiggins, p; Charlie Drayton, sb; Chico Hamilton, d; Marion Abernathy, v.

	Los Angeles, Cal.	26 March 1949
K-5709	Ee-Tid-Ee-Dee	King 4294
K-5710	Ja-Hoosey Baby	King 4319
K-5711	Love Me Or Please Let Me Be	King 4319
K-5712	It's Lonesome Without You	King 4294

LEE YOUNG AND HIS BAND

Vernon 'Geechie' Smith, t; Henry Coker, tb; Marshal Royal, as; Maxwell Davis, ts; Gerald Wiggins, p; John Simmons, sb; Lee Young, d-1/v-2; Chico Hamilton, d-2.

	Los Angeles, Cal.	29 March 1949
4122-2D-1	Seeing Double -1	Capitol 70019
4124-1D-2	Fourth Finger Boogie -1	Capitol 70019
	If I Can't Have You -2	Capitol unissued
	Doodle-Dee-Doo -2	Capitol unissued

HELEN HUMES with MARSHAL ROYAL & HIS ORCHESTRA

John Anderson, Walter (Pete) Candoli, Jack Trainor, t; Britt Woodman, tb; Marshal Royal, as; Henry Bridges, Maxwell Davis, ts/a; Jack McVea, bar; Eddie Beal, p; Jack Marshal, g; Leonard Bibb, sb; Oscar Bradley, d; Helen Humes, v.

	Los Angeles, Cal.	9 May 1950
D-309	Sad Feeling	Discovery 519
D-310	Rock Me To Sleep	Discovery 519
D-311	This Love Of Mine	Discovery 520
D-312	He May Be Yours	Discovery 520

DAMITA JO

John Anderson, Walter (Pete) Candoli, Jack Trainor, t; Murray McEachern, Britt Woodman, Sy Zentner, tb; Buddy Collette, Marshal Royal, as; Henry Bridges, ts; Maxwell Davis, ts/a; Jack McVea, bar; Eddie Beal, p; Jack Marshal, g; Leonard Bibb, sb; Oscar Bradley, d; Damita Jo DeBlanc, v.

	Los Angeles, Cal.	21 May 1950
D-314	Until The Real Thing Comes Along	Discovery 523
D-315	Believe Me	Discovery 521
D-316	Any Time, Any Place, Any Where	Discovery 523
D-317	Here I Am	Discovery 521

RAY CHARLES

Teddy Buckner, t; Marshal Royal, as; Jack McVea, ts; Charles Waller, bar; Ray Charles, p/v; Louis Speiginer, g; Billy Hadnott, sb; Clifton 'Rudy' Pitts, d; LeRoy 'Snake' White, a.

Los Angeles, Cal.	26 May 1950
Th' Ego Song [*a.k.a.* All The Girls In Town]	Swing Time 228
Late In The Evening Blues	Swing Time 228
Someday [*a.k.a.* Blues Is My Middle Name]	Swing Time 229
I'll Do Anything But Work	Swing Time 229

MARSHAL ROYAL AND MAXWELL DAVIS

Marshal Royal, as; Maxwell Davis, ts; unknown, p; unknown, sb; unknown, d.

Los Angeles, Cal.	1951
September In The Rain	Swing Time 251
I've Got The World On A String	Swing Time 251

On the basis of the known movements of the Count Basie Orchestra (see Sheridan, *op. cit.*), which Marshal Royal joined on 5 March 1951, this session (and the session which follows with Ray Charles,) might have taken place either before that date or during the orchestra's residency at the Oasis Club, Los Angeles, from 27 July to 9 August 1951 (but see also notes to the Meredith Howard date of 14 June 1951).

RAY CHARLES

Billy Brooks, Fleming Askew, t; Marshal Royal, Earl Brown, as; Stanley Turrentine, Maurice Simon, ts; Charles Waller, bar; Ray Charles, p/v; Frank McClure, sb; Eddie Pipper, d; band members, v-1.

Los Angeles, Cal.	1951
Kissa Me Baby [*a.k.a.* All Night Long] -1	Swing Time 274
Hey Now	Swing Time 297
The Snow Is Falling [*a.k.a.* I Used To Be So Happy]	Swing Time 326
Misery In My Heart [*a.k.a.* I'm Going Down To The River] -1	Swing Time 326

MEREDITH HOWARD

Art Farmer, t; Marshal Royal, as; Maxwell Davis, ts; Jack McVea, bar; Willard McDaniel, p; Billy Hadnott, sb; Oscar Lee Bradley, d; Meredith Howard, v.

	Los Angeles, Cal.	14 June 1951
3881	Am I To Blame?	Mercury 8233
3882	Goodbye	Mercury 8237
3883	Ten Minutes More	Mercury 8237
3884	Just Kiss Me Once	Mercury 8233

On this date the Count Basie Orchestra was touring and a precise itinerary is not available so it is impossible to say whether the naming of Marshal Royal can be reconciled with the bands movements.

RED CALLENDER SEXTETTE

Marshal Royal, as; Maxwell Davis, ts; Floyd Turnham, bar; Willard McDaniel, p; Red Callender, sb; Chico Hamilton, d; Al Calderone, perc; Mauri Lynn, v-1.

	Hollywood, Cal.	3 August 1951
E1-VB-718-1	Don't Lend No Men No Money -1	Victor unissued
E1-VB-719-1	Fooled Again -1	Victor unissued
E1-VB-720-1	Perdido	Victor 20-4266
E1-VB-721-1	Chico's Boogie	Victor 20-4266

Marshal Royal has been suggested for sessions on the Recorded In Hollywood label by Little Caesar with the Red Callender Sextet (Los Angeles, Cal., 1952) but nothing can be heard on those which have been available to suggest his presence.

PAUL QUINICHETTE AND HIS ORCHESTRA

Joe Newman, t; Henry Coker, tb; Marshal Royal, Ernie Wilkins, as; Paul Quinichette, ts; Charlie Fowlkes, bar; Bobby Tucker, p; Freddie Green, g; Jimmy Lewis, sb-1; Al McKibbon, sb-2; Gus Johnson, d.

	New York City.	July 1952
9346 ·	Bustin' Suds -1	EmArc y EP1-6061
9347	Let's Make It -1	EmArc y EP1-6061
9348	P.Q. Blues -2	EmArcy 16009
9349	Bot, Bot -2	EmArcy 16009

MARSHAL ROYAL

Marshal Royal, as; Ben Webster, ts-1; Bobby Tucker, p; Milt Hinton, sb; Jo Jones, d.

	New York City.	March 1953
9609	Where Is Your Heart (Theme Song From The Moulin Rouge)	Mercury 70140
9610	I Wanna Get Nasty -1	Mercury 70140
9611-2	'S Wonderful -1	EmArcy MG36018
9612	Funky Feelin' Blues	EmArcy MG36018

NELLIE LUTCHER AND HER COMBO

Harry Edison, t; Marshal Royal, as; Nellie Lutcher, p/v; Ulysses Livingston, g; Lee Young, d

Los Angeles, Cal.		25 August 1953
RHCO-10589	Whee, Baby!	Epic LN1108
RHCO-10590	Taking A Chance On Love	Epic LN1108
RHCO-10591	The St. Louis Blues	Epic LN1108

SARAH VAUGHAN

Wendell Culley, Thad Jones, Reunald Jones, Joe Newman; Benny Powell, Bill Hughes, Henry Coker, tb; Marshal Royal, as/cl; Frank Wess, ts/f; Ernie Wilkins, ts; Frank Foster, ts; Charlie Fowlkes, bar; Jimmy Jones, p; Joe Benjamin, sb; Roy Haynes, d.

Carnegie Hall, New York City. 25 September 1954

'S Wonderful	Roulette RE126
Easy To Remember	Roulette RE126
East Of The Sun	Roulette RE126
How Important Can It Be?	Roulette RE126
Make Yourself Comfortable	Roulette RE126
That Old Devil Moon	Roulette RE127
Medley: I Ain't Mad At You/Summertime	Roulette RE127

Marshal Royal also appeared at this concert as a member of the full Count Basie Orchestra

QUINCY JONES AND HIS ORCHESTRA

Jimmy Nottingham, Ernie Royal, Reunald Jones, Joe Newman, t; Jimmy Cleveland, Urbie Green, Sonny Russo, tb; Marshal Royal, Bobby Plater, as; Frank Wess, Sam 'The Man' Taylor, ts; Charlie Fowlkes, bar; Hank Jones, p; Milt Hinton, sb; Gus Johnson, d; Quincy Jones, a/cond.

New York City.	December 1955
Flying Home	Decca unissued
three unknown titles	Decca unissued

ERNIE ANDREWS with BENNY CARTER ORCHESTRA

Harry Edison, Pete Condoli, John Anderson, t; Milt Bernhart, tb; Marshal Royal, Bill Green, as; Buddy Collette, ts/f; Jewell Grant, bar; Gerald Wiggins, p; Barney Kessel, g; Curtis Counce, sb; Jackie Mills, d; Benny Carter, a/cond.

Los Angeles, Cal.	August 1956
In The Dark	Gene Norman Presents GNP28
Song Of The Wanderer	Gene Norman Presents GNP28
Sunset Eyes	Gene Norman Presents GNP28
Peace	Gene Norman Presents GNP28
But Now I Know	Gene Norman Presents GNP28

Make A Present Of You	Gene Norman Presents GNP28
'Round Midnight	Gene Norman Presents GNP28
Lover Come Back To Me	Gene Norman Presents GNP28
Squeeze Me	Gene Norman Presents GNP28
Don't Lead Me On	Gene Norman Presents GNP28

It is difficult to reconcile the quoted date for this session with known movements of the Count Basie Orchestra of which Marshal Royal was a member at this time.

A.K. SALIM AND HIS ORCHESTRA

Jimmy Nottingham, Joe Wilder, t; Marshal Royal, as; Frank Wess, ts; Charlie Fowlkes, bar; Hank Jones, p; Wendell Marshal, sb; Bobby Donaldson, d; Ahmed Khatib Salim, a/dir.

New York City.		1 July 1957
70072	I'll Never Walk Alone	Savoy unissued
70073	If I Loved You	Savoy unissued
70074	June Is Bursting Out All Over	Savoy MG12123
70075	What's The Use Of Wondering	Savoy unissued

Ahmed Khatib Salim was formerly known as Albert Atkinson.

SARAH VAUGHAN

Thad Jones, t/cond; Wendell Culley, Snooky Young, Joe Newman, t; Benny Powell, Al Grey, Henry Coker, tb; Marshal Royal, as/cl; Frank Wess, as/ts/f; Billy Mitchell, Frank Foster, ts; Charlie Fowlkes, bar; Ronnell Bright, p; Freddie Green, g; Richard Davis, sb; Sonny Payne, d; Sarah Vaughan, v.

New York City.		5 January 1958
16931-4	Stardust	Mercury MG20441
16932-12	Doodlin'	Mercury MG20441

COLEMAN HAWKINS Meets THE SAX SECTION

Marshal Royal, Frank Wess, as; Coleman Hawkins, Frank Foster, ts; Charlie Fowlkes, bar; Nat Pierce, p; Freddie Green, g; Eddie Jones, sb; Bobby Donaldson, d.

New York City.	24 April 1958
An Evening At Papa Joe's	World Wide MG20001
There Is Nothing Like A Dame	World Wide MG20001
Ooga Dooga	World Wide MG20001
Thanks For The Misery (take 1)	Savoy SJL1123

	World Wide
Thanks For The Misery	MG20001
I've Grown Accustomed To Her Face	World Wide
	MG20001

JOE NEWMAN AND HIS ORCHESTRA
Joe Newman, t/fh; Marshal Royal, cl/as; Frank Wess, f/as/ts; Romeo Penque, f/ob/ts; Jerry Sanfino, f/ts; Charlie Fowlkes, bar/bcl; George Berg, bcl/ts; Jimmy Jones, p; Freddie Green, g; Ed Jones, sb; Charlie Persip, d.

New York City.	6 May 1958
Nancy	Roulette R52014
My Old Flame	Roulette R52014
You're My Thrill	Roulette R52014
Travlin' Light	Roulette R52014

Joe Newman, t/fh; Marshal Royal, cl/as; Frank Wess, f/as/ts; Romeo Penque, f/ob/ts; Jerry Sanfino, f/ts; Charlie Fowlkes, bar/bcl; George Berg, bcl/ts; Jimmy Jones, p; Freddie Green, g; Ed Jones, sb; Ed Shaugnessy, d.

New York City.	6 May 1958
Old Devil Moon	Roulette R52014
I'll Get By	Roulette R52014
Out Of Nowhere	Roulette R52014
Speak Low	Roulette R52014
Star Eyes	Roulette R52014
Baby, Won't You Please Come Home?	Roulette R52014
Time	Roulette R52014
Lover Man	Roulette R52014

SARAH VAUGHAN
Thad Jones, t/cond; Wendell Culley, Snooky Young, Joe Newman, t; Benny Powell, Al Grey, Henry Coker, tb; Marshal Royal, as/cl; Frank Wess, as/ts/f; Billy Mitchell, Frank Foster, ts; Charlie Fowlkes, bar; Ronnell Bright, p; Freddie Green, g; Richard Davis, sb; Sonny Payne, d; Sarah Vaughan, v.

| New York City. | | 15 December 1958 |
| 17413-17 | Smoke Gets In Your Eyes | Mercury MG20441 |

New York City.		23 December 1958
17423-14	Moonlight In Vermont	Mercury MG20441
17424-16	Cheek To Cheek	Mercury MG20441
17425-1	Missing You	Mercury MG20441
17426-3	Just One Of Those	Mercury MG20441
17427-3	No Count Blues	Mercury MG20441

CHRIS CONNOR
Ernie Royal, Joe Newman, Harry Edison, Snooky Young, t; Al Grey, Frank Rehak, Eddie

Bert, tb; Marshal Royal, Phil Woods, as; Frank Foster, ts; Seldon Powell, ts/f; Charlie Fowlkes, bar; Stan Free, p; Freddie Green, g; Ed Jones, sb; Sonny Payne, d; Chris Connor, v; Ralph Sharon, a.

	New York City.	29 January 1959
A-3338	You And The Night And The Music	Atlantic SD1308
A-3339	Let's Face The Music And Dance	Atlantic SD1308
A-3340	No One Ever Tells You	Atlantic SD1308
A-3341	I'm Just A Lucky So-And-So	Atlantic SD1308

MAXWELL DAVIS

John Anderson, Joe Newman, Snooky Young, Pete Candoli, t; Henry Coker, Dick Nash, Tommy Pedersen, tb; Marshal Royal, Jewell Grant, as; Frank Foster, Frank Wess, ts; Charlie Fowlkes, bar; Milt Raskin, p; Herman Mitchell, g; Ed Jones, sb; Sonny Payne, d; B.B. King, v-1; Maxwell Davis, a/dir.

Los Angeles, Cal.	24 March 1959
Basie Boogie	Crown CLP5111
Every Day I Have The Blues -1	Crown CLP5111
Every Tub	Crown CLP5111
John's Idea	Crown CLP5111
Jumpin' At the Woodside	Crown CLP5111
Lester Leaps In	Crown CLP5111
One O'Clock Jump	Crown CLP5111
Red Bank Boogie	Crown CLP5111
April In Paris	Crown CLP5111

RAY CHARLES with QUINCY JONES ORCHESTRA

Marcus Belgrave, John Hunt, Clark Terry, Ernie Royal, Joe Newman, Snooky Young, t; Melba Liston, Al Grey, Quentin Jackson, Tom Mitchell, tb; Marshal Royal, Frank Wess, as; Dave Newman, Paul Gonsalves, ts; Zoot Sims, ts-1; Billy Mitchell, ts-2; Bennie Crawford, Charlie Fowlkes, bar; Ray Charles, v/p; Freddie Green, g; Edgar Willis, Eddie Jones, sb; Teagle Fleming, Charlie Persip, d; José Mangual, bgs-3; The Raelettes, female v group-4; Quincy Jones, a-5; Ralph Burns, a-6; Al Cohn, a-7; Johnny Acea, a-8; Ernie Wilkins, a-9.

	New York City	23 June 1959
A-3571	Let The Good Times Roll -1, 5	Atlantic SD1312
A-3572	Alexander's Ragtime Band -1, 3, 4, 6	Atlantic SD1312
A-3573	Deed I Do -1, 5	Atlantic SD1312
A-3574	When Your Lover Has Gone -2, 7	Atlantic SD1312
A-3575	Two Years Of Torture -2, 8	Atlantic SD1312
A-3576	It Had To Be You -2, 9	Atlantic SD1312

ERNIE WILKINS AND HIS ORCHESTRA

Ernie Royal, Snooky Young, Thad Jones, Joe Newman, t; Paul Felice, Al Grey, Mickey Graumme, Jack Rains, tb; Marshal Royal, as/cl; Frank Wess, ts/f; Benny Golson, Zoot Sims, ts; Charlie Fowlkes, bar; Jimmy Jones, p; Freddie Green, g; Eddie Jones, sb; Charlie Persip, d; Eddie Costa, vb; Ernie Wilkins, dir.

New York City. 9 December 1959

Somebody Loves Me	Everest
	LPBR5077
Baubles, Bangles And Beads	Everest
	LPBR5077
Gone With The Wind	Everest
	LPBR5077
It Don't Mean A Thing	Everest
	LPBR5077

Ernie Royal, Snooky Young, Dick Williamson, Joe Newman, t; Paul Felice, Al Grey, Mickey Graumme, Jack Rains, tb; Marshal Royal, as/cl; Frank Wess, ts/f Paul Gonsalves, Zoot Sims, ts; Charlie Fowlkes, bar; Jimmy Jones, p; Freddie Green, g; Eddie Jones, sb; Charlie Persip, d; Eddie Costa, vb; Ernie Wilkins, dir.

New York City. 11 January 1960

Broadway	Everest
	LPBR5077
The Surrey With The Fringe On Top	Everest
	LPBR5077
Falling In Love With Love	Everest
	LPBR5077
The Continental	Everest
	LPBR5077
Makin' Whoopee	Everest
	LPBR5077
Stompin' At The Savoy	Everest
	LPBR5077
You're Driving Me Crazy	Everest
	LPBR5077
All Of You	Everest
	LPBR5077

ERNESTINE ANDERSON

Ernie Royal, Nick Travis, Snooky Young, Thad Jones, Joe Newman, t; Benny Powell, Al Grey, Henry Coker, tb; Marshal Royal, Frank Wess, as; Billy Mitchell, Frank Foster, ts; Charlie Fowlkes, bar; Hank Jones, p; Milt Hinton, sb; Charlie Persip, d; Ernestine Anderson, v.

New York City. 1960

19569	Get Out And Get Under	Mercury MG20582
19570	Moanin' Low	Mercury MG20582
19571	Hooray For Love	Mercury MG20582
19572	The Gypsy Goofed	Mercury MG20582

19573	Come Rain Or Come Shine	Mercury MG20582
19574	Tomorrow Mountain	Mercury MG20582
19576	You'll Have To Swing It	Mercury MG20582

The personnel quoted is collective. These titles were recorded at two sessions, one with: 2t; tb; 3 reeds; the other with: 4t; 4tb; 5 reeds.

SAMMY DAVIS, Jr. with JACK PLEIS ORCHESTRA
Ernie Royal, Sonny Cohen, Snooky Young, Thad Jones, Joe Newman, t; Benny Powell, Al Grey, Henry Coker, tb; Marshal Royal, Frank Wess, as; Billy Mitchell, Frank Foster, ts; Charlie Fowlkes, bar; George Rhodes, p; Freddie Green, g; Eddie Jones, sb; Sonny Payne, d; Sammy Davis, Jr., v.

New York City.   1960

Till Then	Decca DL8981
Get On The Right Track	Decca DL8981
I've Heard That Song Before	Decca DL8981
Face To Face	Decca DL8981

Ernie Royal, Sonny Cohen, Snooky Young, Thad Jones, Joe Newman, t; Benny Powell, Al Grey, Henry Coker, Henderson Chambers, tb; Marshal Royal, Frank Wess, as; Billy Mitchell, Frank Foster, ts; Charlie Fowlkes, bar; George Rhodes, p; Freddie Green, g; Eddie Jones, sb; Sonny Payne, d; Sammy Davis, Jr., v; Morty Stevens, dir.

New York City.   1960

I Got A Woman	Decca DL8981
Do Nothin' Till You Hear From Me	Decca DL8981
The Lady Is A Tramp	Decca DL8981
I Got A Right To Sing The Blues	Decca DL8981

Ernie Royal, Sonny Cohen, Snooky Young, Thad Jones, Joe Newman, t; Benny Powell, Al Grey, Henry Coker, tb; Marshal Royal, Eric Dolphy, as; Billy Mitchell, Frank Foster, ts; Charlie Fowlkes, bar; George Rhodes, p; Freddie Green, g; Eddie Jones, sb; Sonny Payne, d; Sammy Davis, Jr., v; Sy Oliver, a.

New York City.   1960

Mess Around	Decca DL8981
This Little Girl Of Mine	Decca DL8981
Gee, Baby, Ain't I Good To You	Decca DL8981
There Is No Greater Love	Decca DL8981

MARSHAL ROYAL
Marshal Royal, as; acc. Gordon Jenkins Orchestra: Hank Jones or Gordon Jenkins, p; Freddie Green, g; Eddie Jones, sb; Sonny Payne, d; string section.

New York City.   14 March 1960

Caravan	Everest BR5087
Ain't Misbehavin'	Everest BR5087
Birth Of The Blues	Everest BR5087

Take The "A" Train	Everest BR5087
When I Grow Too Old To Dream	Everest BR5087
Intermezzo	Everest BR5087
Blue Prelude	Everest BR5087
Battle Royal	Everest BR5087
Goodbye	Everest BR5087
Pagan Love Song	Everest BR5087
Black Coffee	Everest BR5087
Blues For Beverley	Everest BR5087

THE LEIBER-STOLLER BIG BAND

Ernie Royal, Jimmy Nottingham, Joe Newman, Sonny Cohen, t; Frank Rehak, Benny Powell, Henry Coker, Al Grey, tb; Marshal Royal, as; Frank Wess, as/f; Frank Foster, Billy Mitchell, ts; Seldon Powell, ts/f; Charlie Fowlkes, bar; Hank Jones, p; Freddie Green, g; Ed Jones, sb; Sonny Payne, d.

New York City. 15 July 1960

4709	Hound Dog	Atlantic SD8047
4710	Loving You	Atlantic SD8047
4711	Jailhouse Rock	Atlantic SD8047
4712	Poison Ivy	Atlantic SD8047
4713	Yakety Yak	Atlantic SD8047

Ernie Royal, Jimmy Nottingham, Thad Jones, Snooky Young, t; Frank Rehak, Benny Powell, Henry Coker, Al Grey, tb; Marshal Royal, as; Frank Wess, as/f; Frank Foster, Billy Mitchell, ts; Seldon Powell, ts/f; Charlie Fowlkes, bar; Hank Jones, p; Allan Henlon, g; Ed Jones, sb; Sonny Payne, d.

New York City. 18 July 1960

| 4714 | Smokey Joe's Cafe | Atlantic SD8047 |
| 4715 | Charlie Brown | Atlantic SD8047 |

Ernie Royal, Jimmy Nottingham, Joe Newman, Sonny Cohen, t; Frank Rehak, Benny Powell, Henry Coker, Al Grey, tb; Marshal Royal,Frank Wess, as; Frank Foster, Billy Mitchell, ts; Charlie Fowlkes, bar; Ellis Larkins, p; Kenny Burrell, g; Ed Jones, sb; Sonny Payne, d.

New York City. 26 July 1960

4716	Bazoom	Atlantic SD8047
4717	Don't	Atlantic SD8047
4718	Kansas City	Atlantic SD8047
4719	Black Denim Trousers And Motorcycle Boots	Atlantic SD8047
4720	Searchin'	Atlantic SD8047

KING CURTIS AND HIS ORCHESTRA

Ernie Royal, t; Ray Beckenstein or Ray Alonge, fh; Eddie Burt, tb; Garvin Bushell, f/ob; Marshal Royal, cl/as; Haywood Henry, cl/ss/bar; King Curtis Ousley, ts; unknowns, strings

(Mac Cappos, dir); Ernie Hayes, p; Billy Bauer (on some tracks) or Mundell Lowe (on others), g; Lloyd Trotman, b; Panama Francis, d; The Malcolm Dodds Singers (inc. Anita Darian, Christine Spencer, Sue Craven, Ralph Fields, Noah Hopkins, Malcolm Dodds), bgnd v; Sammy Lowe, dir.

Bayside, N.Y.	26 August 1960
Our Love Is Here To Stay	Everest LP5121
Close Your Eyes	Everest LP5121
Azure	Everest LP5121
Offshore	Everest LP5121

Bayside, N.Y.	27 August 1960
The Nearness Of You	Everest LP5121
Unchained Melody	Everest LP5121
My Love Is Your Love	Everest LP5121
It Ain't Necessarily So	Everest LP5121

Bayside, N.Y.	28 August 1960
Sweet And Lovely	Everest LP5121
The Stranger	Everest LP5121
Misty	Everest LP5121
When I Fall In Love	Everest LP5121

RAY CHARLES AND HIS ORCHESTRA

Philip Guilbeau, Thad Jones, Joe Newman, Clark Terry, Snooky Young, t; Henry Coker, Al Grey, Urbie Green, Benny Powell, tb; Marshal Royal, Frank Wess, as; Frank Foster, Billy Mitchell, ts; Charlie Fowlkes, bar; Ray Charles, o/v-1; Freddie Green, g; Eddie Jones, sb; Sonny Payne, d; Quincy Jones, Ralph Burns, a.

	New York City.	26 December 1960
7865	I've Got News For You -1	Impulse! AS2
	From The Heart	Impulse! AS2
	Mister C	Impulse! AS2
	Stompin' Room Only	Impulse! AS2
	Moanin'	Impulse! AS2
	Strike Up The Band	Impulse! AS2

ELLA FITZGERALD

Bobby Bryant, Larry McGuire, Alex Rodriguez, Paul Hubinon, Harry Edison, t; Jay Jay Johnson, Jimmy Cleveland, Mike Wimberley, Britt Woodman, Bill Tole, Alexander Thomas, Thurman Green, tb; Arthur Maebe, frh; Anthony Ortega, Ernie Watts, William Green, f/pic; Marshal Royal, as/cl/f; Henry De Vega, as; Ray Bojorquez, Harold Land, ts; Richard Aplanalp, bar; Tommy Flanagan, p; Joe Sample, o/ep; Herb Ellis or Dennis Budimir, g; Ray Brown, sb; Louie Bellson, d; Modeste Duran, Franzisco De Souxa, bgs/cgs; Vic Feldman or Bobby Hutcherson, vb; Gerald Wilson, a/dir.

Hollywood, Cal.	1970

Sunny	Reprise RS6432
Mas Que Nada	Reprise RS6432
A Man And A Woman	Reprise RS6432
Days Of Wine And Roses	Reprise RS6432
Black Coffee	Reprise RS6432
Tuxedo Junction	Reprise RS6432
I Heard It Through The Grapevine	Reprise RS6432
Don't Dream Of Anybody But Me	Reprise RS6432
Things Ain't What They Used To Be	Reprise RS6432
Willow Weep For Me	Reprise RS6432
Manteca	Reprise RS6432
Just When We're Falling In Love	Reprise RS6432

CLIFFORD COULTER

Harry Edison, John Turk, t; Jimmy Cleveland, tb; Willie Ruff, frh; Bill Perkins, Marshal Royal, as; Plas Johnson, ts; Clifford Coulter, kbrds/g/melodica/v; Sonny Glaze, g; Jimmy Calhoun, eb-1; Ron Beck, d.

	Los Angeles, Cal.	24 May 1971
91214	Before The Morning Comes	Impulse! AS9216
91215	Do It Now, Worry 'Bout It Later -1	Impulse! AS9216

BILL BERRY AND THE L.A. BIG BAND

Bill Berry, c/a; Gene Coe, t/a; Blue Mitchell, Conte Candoli, Jack Sheldon, t; Britt Woodman, Tricky Lofton, Benny Powell, tb; Marshal Royal, Bill Byrne, as; Richie Kamuca, Teddy Edwards, ts; Jack Nimitz, bar/cl; Dave Frishberg, p; Herb Ellis, g; Leroy Vinnegar, sb; Jake Hanna, d; Billy Byers, a.

	Aptos, Cal.	11 May 1974
	Doodle Oodle	Beez 1
	Betty	Beez 1
	Blooze	Beez 1

Bill Berry, c/a; Gene Coe, t/a; Blue Mitchell, Conte Candoli, Cat Anderson, t; Britt Woodman, Tricky Lofton, Benny Powell, tb; Marshal Royal, Bill Byrne, as; Richie Kamuca, Teddy Edwards, ts; Jack Nimitz, bar/cl; Dave Frishberg, p; Herb Ellis, g; Leroy Vinnegar, sb; Jake Hanna, d; Billy Byers, a.

	Concord Jazz Festival, Cal.	2 August 1974
	Smoke Gets Into Your Eyes	Beez 1
	Easter Parade	Beez 1
	Mutton Leg	Beez 1
	Rockin' In Rhythm	Beez 1

BILL BERRY'S L.A. BIG BAND

Bill Berry, Gene Coe, t/a; Blue Mitchell, Cat Anderson, t; Jack Sheldon, t/v-1; Britt Woodman, Jimmy Cleveland, Benny Powell, Tricky Lofton, tb; Marshal Royal, Lanny

Morgan, as; Richie Kamuca, Don Menza, ts; Jack Nimitz, bar/cl; Dave Frishberg, p; Monty Budwig, sb; Frank Capp, d.

| Concord Jazz Festival, Cal. | 1 August 1976 |
| Take The "A" Train | Concord Jazz CJ54 |

Concord Jazz CJ54 is as by **Ernestine Anderson**, but it is not clear whether she sings on this track.

Concord Jazz Festival, Cal.	August 1976
Hello Rev.	Concord Jazz CJ27
Star Crossed Lovers	Concord Jazz CJ27
The Bink And Now	Concord Jazz CJ27
Earl	Concord Jazz CJ27
A Little Song For Mex	Concord Jazz CJ27
Be Your Own Best Friend -1	Concord Jazz CJ27
Tulip Or Turnip	Concord Jazz CJ27
Boy Meets Horn	Concord Jazz CJ27
Cotton Tail	Concord Jazz CJ27

FRANK CAPP/NAT PIERCE BIG BAND

Bill Berry, Gary Grant, Blue Mitchell, Bobby Shew, t; Buster Cooper, Alan Kaplan, Britt Woodman, tb; Bill Green, Marshal Royal, as; Plas Johnson, Richie Kamuca, ts; Quinn Davis, bar; Nat Pierce, p; Al Hendrickson, g; Chuck Berghofer, b; Frank Capp, d; Ernie Andrews, v-1.

King Arthur's, Los Angeles, Cal.	28 August 1976
Avenue "C"	Concord Jazz CJ40
All Heart	Concord Jazz CJ40
Moten Swing	Concord Jazz CJ40
Basie's Back In Town	Concord Jazz CJ40
Mr. Softie	Concord Jazz CCD4040 [CD]
It's Sand, Man	Concord Jazz CCD4040 [CD]
Dickie's Dream	Concord Jazz CJ40
Take The "A" Train	Concord Jazz CJ40
Wee Baby Blues -1	Concord Jazz CJ40
Roll 'Em Pete -1	Concord Jazz CJ40

DAVE FRISHBERG QUINTET

Bob Findley, t; Marshal Royal, as; Dave Frishberg, p/v; Larry Gales, sb; Steve Schaeffer, d.

| Hollywood, Cal. | 25/26 January 1977 |
| Lotus Blossom | Concord Jazz CJ37 |

I Would Do Anything For You	Concord Jazz CJ37
Stevedore Stomp	Concord Jazz CJ37
Violet Blue	Concord Jazz CJ37
Old Man Harlem	Concord Jazz CJ37
Dear Bix	Concord Jazz CJ37

SNOOKY YOUNG-MARSHAL ROYAL SEXTET

Snooky Young, t/fh; Marshal Royal, as; Ross Tompkins, p; Freddie Green, g; Ray Brown, sb; Louie Bellson, d; Scat Man Crothers, v-1.

Hollywood, Cal.	1978
I Let A Song Go Out Of My Heart	Concord Jazz CJ55
Mean Dog Blues -1	Concord Jazz CJ55
Cederay	Concord Jazz CJ55
Limehouse Blues	Concord Jazz CJ55
Cherry	Concord Jazz CJ55
Medley: You've Changed/I'm Confessin'/Come	Concord Jazz CJ55
Sunday/Catch A Star	Concord Jazz CJ55
Should I	Concord Jazz CJ55

BILL BERRY SEPTET

Bill Berry, c; Bill Watrous, tb; Marshal Royal, as; Lew Tabackin, ts/f; Alan Broadbent, p; Chuck Berghofer, b; Nick Ceroli, d.

Los Angeles, Cal.	1978
Betty (Ballad)	Concord Jazz CJ75
Blooze	Concord Jazz CJ75
Royal Garden Blues	Concord Jazz CJ75

THE CAPP/PIERCE JUGGERNAUT

Bill Berry, Al Aarons, Bobby Shew, Frank Szabo, t; Garnett Brown, Buster Cooper, Alan Kaplan, Britt Woodman, tb; Lanny Morgan, Marshal Royal, as; Bob Cooper, Herman Riley, ts; Bill Green, bar; Nat Pierce, p; Ray Pohlman, g; Chuck Berghofer, b; Frank Capp, d; Joe Williams, v-1.

Century Plaza Hotel, New York City.	21 July 1978
Fiesta In Brass	Concord Jazz CJ72
Basie's Deep Fry	Concord Jazz CJ72
Souvenir	Concord Jazz CJ72
Capp This	Concord Jazz CJ72
Tarragon	Concord Jazz CJ72
Swing Shift	Concord Jazz CJ72
Joe's Blues -1	Concord Jazz CJ72
What The World Needs Now Is Love	Concord Jazz CJ72

WARREN VACHÉ SEXTET

Warren Vaché, c/fh; Marshal Royal, as; Nat Pierce, p; Cal Collins, g; Phil Flanigan, sb;

Recording Chronology

Jake Hanna, d.

San Francisco, Cal.   November 1978

It's All Right With Me	Concord Jazz CJ87
Love Locked Out	Concord Jazz CJ87
Taking A Chance On Love	Concord Jazz CJ87
'S Wonderful	Concord Jazz CJ87
I Only Have Eyes For You	Concord Jazz CJ87
More Than You Know	Concord Jazz CJ87
It's You or No One	Concord Jazz CJ87
Jillian	Concord Jazz CJ87
Little White Lies	Concord Jazz CJ87
Too Close For Comfort	Concord Jazz CJ87

MARSHAL ROYAL QUINTET

Marshal Royal, as; Nat Pierce, p; Cal Collins, g; Monte Budwig, sb; Jake Hanna, d.

Venice, Cal.   December 1978

Little Girl Blue	Concord Jazz CJ88
I've Got The World On A String	Concord Jazz CJ88
Who Can I Turn To?	Concord Jazz CJ88
Jitterbug Waltz	Concord Jazz CJ88
Jump	Concord Jazz CJ88
Stardust	Concord Jazz CJ88
Li'l Darlin'	Concord Jazz CJ88
My Ideal	Concord Jazz CJ88

THE CONCORD ALL STARS

Snooky Young, t-1; Marshal Royal, as; Ross Tompkins, p; Cal Collins, g; Ray Brown, sb; Jake Hanna, d.

Concord Jazz Festival, Cal.   August 1979

Moten Swing -1	Concord Jazz CJ117
Don't Get Around Much Anymore -1	Concord Jazz CJ117
Willow Weep For Me	Concord Jazz CJ117
Exactly Like You -1	Concord Jazz CJ117
Pavilion Blues -1	Concord Jazz CJ117

Marshal Royal is not on other titles from this session.

ZOOT SIMS

Bobby Bryant, Oscar Brashear, Al Aarons, Earl Gardner, t; Jay Jay Johnson, Britt Woodman, Grover Mitchell, Benny Powell, tb; Marshal Royal, as; Frank Wess, as/f; Zoot Sims, Plas

Johnson, Buddy Collette, ts; Jimmy Rowles, p; John Collins, g; Andy Simpkins, sb; Grady Tate, d; Benny Carter, a/cond.

Hollywood, Cal.	14 August & 10/11
	December 1979
In A Mellotone	Pablo 2312.120
I Got It Bad And That Ain't Good	Pablo 2312.120
It Don't Mean A Thing	Pablo 2312.120
I Let A Song Go Out Of My Heart	Pablo 2312.120
Black Butterfly	Pablo 2312.120

MARSHAL ROYAL QUINTET

Marshal Royal, as; Monty Alexander, p; Cal Collins, g; Ray Brown, sb; Jimmie Smith,d.

Hollywood, Cal.	March 1980
Mean To Me	Concord Jazz CJ125
I'll Be Comin' Home	Concord Jazz CJ125
Avalon	Concord Jazz CJ125
Just Squeeze Me (But Don't Tease Me)	Concord Jazz CJ125
Things Ain't What They Used To Be	Concord Jazz CJ125
Teach Me Tonight	Concord Jazz CJ125
Royal Riff	Concord Jazz CJ125
I Got It Bad And That Ain't Good	Concord Jazz CJ125
Everything Happens To Me	Concord Jazz CJ125

JUDY CARMICHAEL QUINTET

Marshal Royal, as; Judy Carmichael, p; Freddie Green, g; Red Callender, sb; Harold Jones, d.

Hollywood, Cal.	4 & 29 April 1980
Christopher Columbus	Progressive PRO7065
Ja-Da	Progressive PRO7065
Honeysuckle Rose	Progressive PRO7065
Ain't Misbehavin'	Progressive

Recording Chronology

	PRO7065
I Ain't Got Nobody	Progressive
	PRO7065
(I Would Do) Anything For You	Progressive
	PRO7065

Marshal Royal is not on other titles from this session.

KENNY BURRELL

Oscar Brashear, Snooky Young, t; Marshal Royal, Matt Catingub, Jerome Richardson, Don Menza, reeds; Patrice Rushen, Pete Jolly, p; Kenny Burrell, g; Andrew Simpkins, b; Shelly Manne, d; Moacir Santos, perc.

Los Angeles, Cal.	27/28 May 1980
Night In Tunisia	Audio Source
	ASD1
Mood Indigo	Audio Source
	ASD1
St. Louis Blues	Audio Source
	ASD1
'Round Midnight	Audio Source
	ASD1
When The Saints Go Marching In	Audio Source
	ASD1
Naima	Audio Source
	ASD1
Struttin' With Some Barbecue	Audio Source
	ASD1
A Child Is Born	Audio Source
	ASD1
Lush Life	Audio Source
	ASD1

The above personnel is collective and it is not known on which tracks Marshal Royal actually plays.

THE CAPP/PIERCE ORCHESTRA

John Audino, Al Aarons, Frank Szabo, Warren Luening, t; Buster Cooper, Alan Kaplan, George Bohannon, Mel Wanzo, tb; Bill Green, ss/bar; Joe Roccisano, Marshal Royal, as; Pete Christlieb, Bob Cooper, ts; Nat Pierce, p; Ray Pohlman, g; Bob Maize, b; Frank Capp, d; Ernie Andrews, v-1.

Hollywood, Cal.	October/
	November 1981
Little Pony	Concord Jazz
	CJ183
I Remember Clifford	Concord Jazz

	CJ183
New York Shuffle	Concord Jazz
	CJ183
You Are So Beautiful	Concord Jazz
	CJ183
Things Ain't What They Used To Be	Concord Jazz
	CJ183

John Audino, Al Aarons, Snooky Young, Bill Berry, t; Buster Cooper, Alan Kaplan, George Bohannon, Mel Wanzo, tb; Bill Green, ss/bar; Jackie Kelso, Marshal Royal, as; Pete Christlieb, Bob Efford, ts; Nat Pierce, p; Ray Pohlman, g; Bob Maize, b; Frank Capp, d; Ernie Andrews, v-1.

Hollywood, Cal.	October/
	November 1981
One For Marshal	Concord Jazz
	CJ183
Chops, Fingers And Sticks	Concord Jazz
	CJ183
Medley: Parker's Mood/Word From Bird	Concord Jazz
	CJ183
Charade	Concord Jazz
	CJ183

"QUARTET"

Al Aarons, t; Benny Powell, tb; Marshal Royal, cl/as; Jerome Richardson, ts/cl; J. Leonard Oxley, p; Allen Jackson, sb; Rudy Collins, d; Armelia McQueen, v-1; Luther Henderson, a.

unknown location	c. 1980/81
Opening Title Music	Gramavision
	GR1020
Five-O-Nine	Gramavision
	GR1020
Blues For H.J.	Gramavision
	GR1020
Black King Foxtrot	Gramavision
	GR1020
Full Time Lover	Gramavision
	GR1020
In The Country	Gramavision
	GR1020
Pars	Gramavision
	GR1020
Au Bal Musette	Gramavision
	GR1020

Five-O-Nine -1	Gramavision GR1020
Full Time Lover -1	Gramavision GR1020
Maggie's Trot	Gramavision GR1020
Quartet Tango	Gramavision GR1020
End Title Music	Gramavision GR1020

This is the original soundtrack music for the Merchant Ivory Productions film *Quartet*, dir James Ivory, a Franco-British co-production. Location-shooting in Paris took place in 1980, but the soundtrack may have been recorded later and in the U.S.A. It is assumed that the two duplicated titles are vocal and non-vocal versions. In the film, *Pars* has a vocal, performed on screen by the actress Isabelle Adjani, but it is not known whether she performs on the soundtrack, or whether the version on the album is vocal.

ELLA FITZGERALD
Al Aarons, t; Bill Watrous, tb; David Allen Duke, Gale Robinson, Joe Meyer, Richard Klein, frh; Hubert Laws, Wilbur Schwartz, Ronnie Lang, Bill Green, f; Marshal Royal, as; Bob Coope, ts; Jerome Kessler, Dennis Karmazyn, Christine Ermacoff, Barbara Jane, Jane Hunter, Nancy Stein, Robert L. Martin, Frederick Seykora, Judy Perett, vc; Jimmy Rowles, p; Art Hillery, o; Joe Pass, g; Tommy Tedesco, g-1; Jim Hughart, b; Shelly Manne, d; Nelson Riddle, a.

Hollywood, Cal.	4-5 February 1982
I Wonder Where Our Love Has Gone -1	Pablo 2312-138
Don't Be That Way	Pablo 2312-138
God Bless The Child	Pablo 2312-138
You're Driving Me Crazy	Pablo 2312-138
Good-Bye -1	Pablo 2312-138
Any Old Time	Pablo 2312-138
Autumn In New York -1	Pablo 2312-138
The Best Is Yet To Come	Pablo 2312-138
Deep Purple -1	Pablo 2312-138
Somewhere In The Night -1	Pablo 2312-138

THE GENE HARRIS ALL STAR BIG BAND
John Faddis, Conte Candoli, Frank Szabo, Bobby Bryant, t; Charlie Loper, Bill Watrous, Garnett Brown, tb; Bill Reichenbach, btb; Marshal Royal, Bill Green, as; Bob Cooper, Plas Johnson, ts; Jack Nimitz, bar; Gene Harris, p; Herb Ellis, g; Ray Brown, sb; Jeff Hamilton, d; Frank Wess, a-1; John Clayton, a-2

Burbank, Cal.	March 1987

Recording Chronology

      Captain Bill -2   Concord Jazz
CJ337

      Night Mist -1   Concord Jazz
CJ337

      Blue And Sentimental -1   Concord Jazz
CJ337

      Riled Up -1   Concord Jazz
CJ337

      (I'm Afraid) The Masquerade Is Over -1   Concord Jazz
CJ337

Snooky Young, Conte Candoli, Frank Szabo, Bobby Bryant, t; Charlie Loper, Thurman Green, Garnett Brown, tb; Bill Reichenbach, btb; Marshal Royal, Jackie Kelso, as; Bob Cooper, Plas Johnson, ts; Jack Nimitz, bar; Gene Harris, p; Herb Ellis, g; James Leary, sb; Jeff Hamilton, d; Frank Wess, a-1; Mickey Tucker, a-2.

    Burbank, Cal.   June 1987

      Swingin' The Blues -2   Concord Jazz
CJ337

      When Did You Leave Heaven -1   Concord Jazz
CJ337

      Dejection Blues -1   Concord Jazz
CJ337

FRANK WESS-HARRY EDISON ORCHESTRA

Harry Edison, Raymond Brown, Al Aarons, Snooky Young, Joe Newman, t; Al Grey, Grover Mitchell, Benny Powell, Michael Grey, tb; Curtis Peagler, Marshal Royal, as; Billy Mitchell, ts; Frank Wess, ts/f; Bill Ramsey, bar; Ronnell Bright, p; Ted Dunbar, g; Eddie Jones, b; Gregg Field, d.

    Kani-Hoken Hall, Tokyo, Japan.   November 1989

      Jumpin' At The Woodside   Concord Jazz
CCD4420 [CD]

      The Very Thought Of You   Concord Jazz
CCD4420 [CD]

      Blue On Blue   Concord Jazz
CCD4420 [CD]

      All Riled Up   Concord Jazz
CCD4420 [CD]

      This Is All I Ask   Concord Jazz
CCD4420 [CD]

      I Wish I Knew   Concord Jazz
CCD4420 [CD]

      Whirly Bird   Concord Jazz
CCD4420 [CD]

Li'l Darlin'	Concord Jazz
	CCD4420 [CD]
Dejection Blues	Concord Jazz
	CCD4420 [CD]
Battle Roya	Concord Jazz
	CCD4420 [CD]
One O'Clock Jump	Concord Jazz
	CCD4420 [CD]

ERNIE WILKINS & ALL STARS BAND

Snooky Young, Benny Bailey, t; Art Farmer, t/fh; Grover Mitchell, Curtis Fuller, tb; Alvin Batiste, cl; Marshal Royal, as/cl; Frank Wess, ts/f; Ernie Wilkins, ts/a; Joe Henderson, ts; Ronnie Cuber, bar; James Williams, p; Jimmy Woode, sb; Charlie Persip, d.

Paris		May 1990
	Johnny Come Lately	Birdology
		519.346-2
	The Mooche	Birdology
		519.346-2
	Sphisticated Lady	Birdology
		519.346-2
	Kinda Dukish	Birdology
		519.346-2
	My Little Brown Book	Birdology
		519.346-2
	Things Ain't What They Used To Be	Birdology
		519.346-2
	Good Queen Bess	Birdology
		519.346-2
	Don't Get Around Much Anymore	Birdology
		519.346-2
	Isfahan	Birdology
		519.346-2

MEL TORMÉ with FRANK WESS-HARRY EDISON ORCHESTRA

Harry Edison, Raymond Brown, Pete Minger, Joe Newman, t; Al Grey, Grover Mitchell, Benny Powell, tb; Curtis Peagler, Marshal Royal, as; Billy Mitchell, Frank Wess, ts; Bill Ramsey, bar; John Campbell, p; Ted Dunbar, g; Bob Maize, sb; Donny Osborne, d; Mel Tormé, v.

Concord Pavilion, Concord, Cal.		August 1990
	Down For Double	Concord Jazz
		CCD4433 [CD]
	You're Driving Me Crazy (What Did I Do)	Concord Jazz
		CCD4433 [CD]

171

Sent For You Yesterday (And Here You Come Today)   Concord Jazz
CCD4433 [CD]

ERNESTINE ANDERSON with MARSHAL ROYAL AND THE GENE HARRIS QUARTET
Marshal Royal, as; Gene Harris, p; Ed Bickert, g; Lynn Seaton, sb; Harold Jones, d; Ernestine Anderson, v.

Concord Pavilion, Concord, Cal.	18 August 1990
Skylark	Concord Jazz
	CCD4454 [CD]

FRANK WESS SEPTET
Pete Minger, fh; Marshal Royal, as; Frank Wess, ts/f; Rick Wilkins, ts; Gerald Wiggins, p; Lynn Seaton, sb/v; Harold Jones, d.

Concord Pavilion, Concord, Cal.	18 August 1990
The Blues Walk	Concord Jazz
	CCD4452 [CD]
Lush Life	Concord Jazz
	CCD4452 [CD]
Don't Get Around Much Anymore	Concord Jazz
	CCD4452 [CD]
Easy Living	Concord Jazz
	CCD4452 [CD]
Just Squeeze Me (But Don't Tease Me)	Concord Jazz
	CCD4452 [CD]
Broadway	Concord Jazz
	CCD4452 [CD]

NONI BERNARDI BIG BAND
Bill Berry, c; Frank Szabo, John Audino, Pete Candoli, t; Dick Nash, Joe Howard, Lloyd Ulyate, tb; Don Raffell, Les Robinson, Willie Schwartz, Marshal Royal, Don Lodice, Bill Green, Abe Most, reeds; Ray Sherman, p; Red Callender, sb; Frank Capp, d; Ernani 'Noni' Bernardi, dir.

Los Angeles, Cal.	late 1980s or early 1990s
Don't Be That Way	Un-numbered
	NTSC video
Back Bay Shuffle	Un-numbered
	NTSC video
Jersey Bounce	Un-numbered
	NTSC video
Swanee River	Un-numbered
	NTSC video
Begin The Beguine	Un-numbered

172

Recording Chronology

	NTSC video
Jumpin' At The Woodside	Un-numbered
	NTSC video
Don't Get Around Much Anymore	Un-numbered
	NTSC video
String Of Pearls	Un-numbered
	NTSC video
In The Mood	Un-numbered
	NTSC video
Song Of India	Un-numbered
	NTSC video
Opus One	Un-numbered
	NTSC video
April In Paris	Un-numbered
	NTSC video

This video, entitled *The Way It Was*, is produced by Noni Bernardi Enterprises. There may be additional tracks to those listed.

Index

Index